D0099950

RECIPES
from a
SPANISH
VILLAGE

PEPITA ARIS

Special photography by
Linda Burgess

For my mother, who gave me my name
and bought a house in Spain

Copyright © 1990 by Pepita Aris

All rights reserved. No part of this publication may be
reproduced or transmitted in any form or by any means,
electronic or mechanical, including photocopy, recording, or
any information storage and retrieval system, without
permission in writing from the publisher.

Project Editor: Cortina Butler
Art Director: Mary Evans
Edited by: Denise Bates
Designer: Christine Wood
Picture Research: Nadine Bazar
Production: Julia Golding
Home Economist: Jane Suthering
Assisted by Meg Jansz
Photographic Stylist: Debbie Patterson
Painted Pottery: Barbara Mullarney Wright
Line Artwork: Conny Jude

First published in 1990 by
Stoddart Publishing Co. Limited
34 Lesmill Road
Toronto, Canada
M3B 2T6

Published in Great Britain by
Conran Octopus Limited
37 Shelton Street
London WC2H 9HN

Canadian Cataloguing in Publication Data
Aris, Pepita.
  Recipes from a Spanish village

ISBN 0-7737-2451-6

1. Cookery, Spanish. I. Title.

TX723.5.S7A75 1990   641.5946   C90-094586-9

Typeset by Elite Typesetting Techniques, Southampton, England
Printed and bound in Hong Kong

CONTENTS

INTRODUCTION

S PANISH FOOD EMBRACES A WORLD of sun and color. It has the immediacy of food picked only when it is ripe, or cooked and eaten almost directly from the sea. It is honest food, bringing a few local products together to make a dish. And it is, above all, simple food, but cooked carefully, with an understanding of the very best way to exploit what it offers.

Spain is an unexplored territory for most cooks, who have no more than a casual European vacation aquaintance, perhaps. But the world of Spanish villages is probably unknown, and your kitchen shelf is unlikely to contain a book on Spanish fish cooking, or the cooking of any particular region of Spain. Unlike the food of Italy and France, for instance, Spanish food, with a couple of famous exceptions, is surprisingly undiscovered even within Europe.

This is real food, village food – direct, simple and tasty. The recipes are suggested by the flavors, textures and colors of the ingredients themselves, and are not distorted by decoration or artifice in any way. Their secret lies in years of direct experience, experience which has shown that certain things combine in a particularly successful way. *No se admiten trampas en la cocina*, the Spaniards would say – no tricks to disguise indifferent food in the kitchen.

Occasionally the ingredients for some of these recipes may require a little hunting down. But while a few Spanish recipes take time, it is fortunately not *your* time. The dishes are quickly prepared and you can then sit back and wait while they cook: there is little fussing around. Spanish dishes also fall into a natural rhythm. One dish may leave you with exactly the ingredient needed – such as cooked chickpeas, or boiled ham – to complete the next one in Spanish style. The Spaniards also like single things on a plate. This is a relief from the tyranny of having to make lots of dishes for each main course, while a sequence of salads and other dishes is also easier to serve.

The length of some recipes does not mean they are difficult. They may often be quicker to cook than to explain, and readers familiar with foods like artichokes, or salt cod, can skip through the explanations which I have offered for those who are meeting these foods for the first time.

Certain things are impossible to make well here without the native fish, shellfish and sometimes vegetables, and every cook worth his or her salt makes a contribution to the recipe cooked. But I do like recipes to respect their origins, and not to get away from what they are – a picnic dish to eat in the fields, a fisherman's stew, a Sunday pot containing the best the farmyard has to offer. I don't like them sieved, decorated and the like, with no respect for the origin or nature of the dish.

I have a prejudice in favor of the natural, original way of cooking traditional things too – but speeded along by using modern machinery. I have tried here to present the old tastes, refined perhaps, but not disguised or obliterated by modern ideas of what tastes good. Some recipes – very few – have been slightly rethought to make them lighter or healthier, but they are not repackaged for the international market.

Spanish cooking is largely regional cooking, based on the produce of an immediate area. Although I have had a house in one of the prettiest villages of Andalusia for nearly twenty years, these recipes come from all over a country that varies quite markedly. Many generalizations have been made about Spain, the famous one being that the cooking is like the climate: "In the north they stew, on the plains they roast and in the south they fry." Different provinces, too, are known for their different talents. The Basques are knowledgeable cooks; the Catalans experimental and adventurous, their cooking is progressive and dazzling, with a capacity to take you by surprise just when you thought you knew it. But all over Spain you will find color on a plate and common sense about the food that is available turned into an art.

I can do no more than Richard Ford, the 19th-century traveler, and "skim the subject, which is indeed fat and unctuous." I hope you will go to Spain and seek out its traditional recipes there. Meanwhile, experience some of its pleasures by cooking them yourself.

PEPITA ARIS

INSIDE A SPANISH PANTRY

AGUARDIENTE

"Toothwater" it is not, though that is how Richard Ford referred to it, some 130 years ago. It is usually a colorless *eau-de-vie*, the anise-flavored kind being popular for cooking, but the term includes any distilled liquor. *Aguardiente de orujo* is a grape brandy, like *marc*, made from skins and pips.

ALMONDS AND HAZELNUTS

Almendras were introduced by the Moors, and almonds are basic to most cookies and many Spanish sauces. Toasted almonds and hazelnuts, *avellanas*, are exquisite and partner sherry well. Toast them in a low oven at about 300° F for 20 minutes to bring out their flavor.

ARTICHOKES

Alcachofas are served whole or the bases only may be prepared (mainly for salads). Hearts (whole immature artichokes) and bases are both sold canned. To prepare the base see page 103; to cook and eat whole see page 74.

BACALAO

Cod is not a Mediterranean fish, but the Spaniards immediately took to salted, dried cod. The phrase *cortar el bacalao*, "first choice at the *bacalao*," means to be "top dog." Indispensable as a Lenten food, and associated with Good Friday, it has become a year-round favorite, though it looks stiff and rather unappealing when raw.

Bacalao increases in weight by half when soaked, but this is lost again in discarded bones and skin. Soak the fish for 24 hours – longer if it is not to be cooked in any liquid – preferably under running water, otherwise change the water 2–3 times. Remove all skin, bones, fins and badly discolored flesh. The thick center cuts are prized most highly, and should not taste salty after proper preparation.

BEANS

Alubias, in a wide selection of colors, are dried beans, and each area of Spain has its own local favorite. Introduced from America, these beans alleviated what was at that time a tedious diet, based on broad or fava beans, *habas*, and chickpeas (garbanzos). The nearest bean to *faba*, the white bean of Galicia, is the butter bean. All dried beans have a natural affinity with salted meat.

Fresh beans are also eaten, of course: *pochas* are podded fresh white beans, and fresh green beans are *judías verdes*. Soak dried beans overnight in cold water, or for 1 hour in boiling water. They more than double in weight after cooking. Modern varieties, however, do not need the long cooking of traditional recipes, and can break up disagreeably. Fresh and soaked kidney beans will both cook in around 1 hour.

BRANDY

Coñac is cheap in Spain and is used as the French might use Martini, to bolster wine sauces. The big seller is the inappropriately named Soberano, which is less sweet. But the fashion is increasingly for sweeter, caramelized after-dinner brandies: like Veterano, whose cut-out bull advertisements so contribute to the southern skyline of Spain, and Magno, which is smooth and aromatic.

BREAD

Spanish bread is white and of excellent quality, freshly baked every day, and sold first thing in the morning as rolls, under names like *bollo* or *chica*, "little girl," and later in the day as the larger *pan*. Whole wheat bread, and some rye or corn bread, can be found in the northwest corner of the country.

Bread is the standard accompaniment to food, in a country where few dishes are paired. Bread is also eaten as a *bocadillo*, a crusty roll sandwich, with olive oil replacing butter. The *cocas* of Mallorca are the nearest thing to an Italian pizza.

Stale bread is used as a thickener for sauces, for it will hold a little fat in suspension; the result is light and not greasy. *Torrijas* are a children's treat: stale bread dipped in milk, then egg-coated, fried and sugared.

BUTIFARRA

A common white sausage in Catalonia and Mallorca, it is made of pork, tripe and pine nuts and spiced with cinnamon and cumin. It is good grilled or broiled. There are also black *butifarrones* – a nickname for the middle classes in their black coats.

CARDOON

The *cardo* is popular in Navarre, a relative of the globe artichoke but less well known. The stalks are boiled and eaten with butter or béchamel sauce.

CHARD

Acelga is an old vegetable found around the Mediterranean. The glossy dark leaves and bright white stalks can be eaten together, but are most often separated. Spinach can be substituted for the leaves of chard.

CHEESE

Mountains and cheese go together, and ewes' milk cheeses are found all over Europe's most mountainous country. Goats' milk cheeses are made in both the south and north, but only in the wetter north can one find cheese from cows' milk. Most cheeses are still unpasteurized.

The most famous cheese, and the only one exported in any quantity, is Manchego. It is best known in a black rind. Spanish cheeses vary widely in the course of aging, and Manchego may be mild and quite soft, or strong and hard. Because it is made of ewes' milk it is expensive – more so than Parmesan, which makes the best substitute. Manchego-style cheeses stored in olive oil are a good buy, as they age without drying.

The most famous blue cheese is Cabrales, and the similar Picón, from the Picos de Europa where it is made. Creamy, blue-veined and sold wrapped in leaves, it is the Spanish Roquefort: a gourmet treat.

Fresh cheeses are made around the country, like *queso de Burgos*, widely available in Spain and eaten as a dessert with honey. From Galicia the creamy *tetilla* is famous for the name "titty,"

SAVIA DE LA VIDA ES EL ZUMO DE LA FRUTA DE ESPAÑA

Bevorzugt SPANIENS Edelobst.
Demandez partout les Fruits d'ESPAGNE.
Eat more SPANISH fruits.

and its gentle breast shape.

Smoked cheeses include one from Roncal, with tiny holes, and the shiny, amber-colored San Simón, which looks like a ripe pear.

Soft cheeses are eaten with fruit or honey as a dessert, but firm and hard ones are most popular plain, with bread, at either end of a meal. Cooking with cheese is not a Spanish habit, though the spread of Italian pasta dishes in the 19th century introduced cheese sauces. Cheese is grated over baked vegetables like eggplants and breaded fried cheese, *queso frito*, is a popular *tapa*.

CHICKPEAS

These *garbanzos* are "the potato of the land," commented Richard Ford. They are sold dried or *en remojo*, soaked; are eaten everywhere; and are honored in Madrid with names like *gabrieles*, angels, and *trompitos*, trumpets.

They are also sold already cooked and salted, particularly during festivals, as a *tapa* and for giving to children.

Soak overnight in three times their volume of cold water, or in boiling water for 1 hour. I find modern varieties cook in an hour, but they are one of the few legumes that do not spoil if overcooked and are intact after $2\frac{1}{2}$ hours. They reheat well.

CHILIES

Spanish cooking is distinguished by its subtle use of capsicums. The smallest and hottest is *guindilla*, lending heat to the dishes of the northwest. A little cayenne is a simple substitute.

A sweet chili pepper that is not hot is an unfamiliar idea, but the *choricero* has had great influence on Spanish cooking. You can see it drying in red bunches, hung from every balcony in villages like Laguardia in Rioja, during the fall. It gives their name, plus color and piquancy, to *chorizo* sausages, and is an essential ingredient of Basque dishes *a la vizcaina*. Another sweet chili pepper is the *ñora*, called *romesco* in Catalonia (see page 88).

CHORIZO

Chorizos are sausages containing paprika from the *choricero* pepper. There are two main types.

Cured *chorizos* are the larger, about 2 inches in diameter, and are sliced and eaten raw on bread as a *tapa*. Best known are those from Rioja, and from Pamplona. They are fine-flavored but chewy, though the Pamplona *chorizo* is more finely textured. A few are exported from Spain.

Cooking *chorizos* are a local affair and may be smoked or fresh, but will always be fatty. "A little capsicum-red fellow . . . with some garlic juice – not a flood, but a flavoring breath," this is *the* scarlet sausage, and the heavy paprika content leaches out in cooking, to color potatoes or soups red. *Chorizos* linked by scarlet string will be far hotter than others with plain string.

Cooking *chorizos* are made all over the country, but those from Extremadura and Asturias are most famous. For *cocido madrileño* (see page 104), the first choice is *chorizo* from Cantimpalos in Segovia. *Chistorra* is a thin red sausage from Navarre which looks like *chorizo*.

Spanish, Mexican and Italian grocery stores are the best places to find paprika sausages. For frying, fresh garlic sausages make acceptable substitutes, but for boiling, look for smoked sausages. There are also supermarket imitations, adequate but not as good as the real thing, and smoked sausages from Eastern Europe like *kabanos*.

CIDER

Cider apples may have originated on the Black Sea, but the Basques feel they perfected the drink. It is strongly alcoholic and in the *sidrería* shops you can drink all the cider you wish, for a small fee, and eat in the intervals. Hard cider is made in wet Asturias, too, and here it replaces wine.

CINNAMON

The association of cinnamon with lamb and poultry dates from Moorish times – originally for its antiseptic properties. Now *canela* is much used for all Spanish sweets, including their favorite cookies and ice creams. Cinnamon is partnered with chocolate, rather than vanilla, for the Spaniards missed the Mexican association of these two altogether.

FAT

Though the Spaniards are Mediterranean, and have always liked olive oil, they adopted lard, *saim*, or pig's fat under the influence of northern barbarians. Because it made the food richer, pork fat has become synonymous with abundance. Butter is used in Galicia and the Pyrenees, but it is not traditional elsewhere.

The combination of olive oil and fat is a very basic one in Spanish cooking. Pork fat, incidentally, has half the cholesterol of butter. TOCINO (see page 16), sold as blocks of hard fat, and soft *manteca de cerdo*, encased in a plastic sausage, are both used for frying. *Manteca colorada* (see page 28), fat colored with paprika (but not necessarily with added meat), is typical of Seville and Cordoba. It is used for frying and is also spread on toast for breakfast.

A by-product of pork fat is crackling. Called *chicharro*, this is sold as a snack at corner stores.

I find the easiest non-vegetable fat, and the best for flavor, is rendered fat from poultry. Corn-fed chickens give off a considerable amount (of vegetable origin, but tasting of poultry), while duck fat keeps well.

GARLIC

Garlic is fundamental to Spanish cooking, although wrongly thought to dominate it. Its importance is illustrated by the phrase *estar en el ajo*, "in the garlic," meaning to be "in the know." Used raw or cooked, garlic has two quite different flavors, the first pungent, the second suggestive. A dish *al ajillo* is flavored with chopped garlic, while *ajo* means whole cloves appear, and they may be eaten like white beans, made mild by long cooking.

Few books bother to explain that when garlic is the first ingredient to go

into the skillet, it is there only to flavor the oil, and is then automatically discarded. Otherwise the garlic turns to "tea leaves."

Garlic is an essential part of *sofrito*, that sequence of soft onion, with garlic and chopped parsley added, that is at the base of so many Spanish rice dishes and sauces. It is also part of a *picada*, a thickening mixture for a sauce, which is added at the end of cooking. Its most famous use, though, is in *alioli* (see pages 54 and 101). The original sauce, which dates back to Roman times in Spain, was just garlic in oil, used as a condiment. Nowadays it is frequently made with egg yolks and served with grilled meat and fried fish, or added to soups on serving.

HAM AND CURED MEATS

Spanish raw ham is very famous (see JAMÓN SERRANO), but cooked ham and bacon are also sold. Small quantities of ham are frequently needed in Spanish cooking and I prefer this cut from a large piece of raw smoked ham or meaty hock. The latter is a small, cheap supermarket cut, with a useful bone for Spanish-style recipes. It can be split into two or three pieces, which can then be frozen. Smoked pork chops are easy to buy and, being thicker than bacon, they cube neatly. You can render the fat scraps for frying.

In Spain various types of cured pork are on sale. The famous *lacón* of Galicia is the cured front leg of the pig, and more esoteric parts like salted ears, tails and feet are all appreciated for the flavor they give to stews.

There are also *salones*: cured meat from lamb, kid and beef. The best known of these is *cecina*, which is salted, air-dried beef and hence called "bull's ham."

JAMÓN SERRANO

A gourmet feast by itself, this raw ham is much in demand. It has a beautiful chewy texture served in thin slices on bread, and is also used for cooking. Traditionally *serrano* is carved with the grain, along, rather than into, the ham but less finely than Italian *prosciutto*, which is the nearest substitute.

The most famous hams are cured where there are winter snows, hence their name of "mountain" hams. Jabugo in Huelva and Trevélez in Granada are famous in the south, though the Duc de St. Simon, in the 19th century, thought the hams of Montánchez in Extremadura were the most exquisite thing he had tasted, and hams from Lérida and Teruel, both in the east, are also well known.

The best *jamon serrano* comes from the black and red Iberian pig, which roams half-wild in the mountains, eating acorns, which marbles the flesh with flavorful fat. Lesser raw hams, from white pigs, are much leaner and so are widely eaten.

The pigs are slaughtered in the fall, and the hams packed in salt for 8 – 10 days, then hung in airy rooms upstairs for the 6 winter months. When the weather turns warm, the hams begin to sweat salt, which is allowed to happen for one week. They are then moved to cool cellars and hung there for the 6 warm months.

Jamón is also used for cooking, as it has to be trimmed every now and then for slicing. Old bones, called *añejos*, are sold for boiling.

LOMO EMBUCHADO

A smoked, pink, pig's loin cured whole in a sausage casing, it tastes like good ham. Sliced into neat rounds, it is a delicious, but expensive, form of cold meat, eaten on bread as a *tapa*.

El aceite Español es puro de Oliva

LONGANIZA

A thin, hard, bland sausage, like a somewhat fatty salami inside, *longaniza* hangs in a wonderful hank around and around its own wooden bar. It is used for cooking, and the word may cover other varieties of sausage.

MORCILLA

A black sausage, in links or occasionally rings, it is dark both because it contains pig's blood and because it is smoked. This, and the unusually large amount of onion in it, give it a rich flavor. It may also contain pine nuts, rice and cinnamon.

The most famous *morcillas* come from Extremadura and Asturias, where they are a principal ingredient of *fabada* (see page 106). They are always cooked. The best substitute is a good blood sausage.

There is a second type, called *morcilla*

dulce, which can be eaten as a *tapa*. The spicy sweetness and dark color, with a rich, tongue-clinging creamy fat, make it the nearest thing to eating Christmas plum pudding.

MUSHROOMS

Champiñones, from the French, are cultivated mushrooms, but the Spaniards prefer *setas*, wild ones, and *hongos*, a smaller category of fungus. From April, when the mild *moixernons* first appear, to the end of the fall, mushroom picking is a national hobby. *Boletos*, cèpes, and *rossinyols*, chanterelles, are the most popular. Best-known and, dare I say, slightly overrated, are *rovellons* (see page 66). Wild mushrooms are usually cooked simply, or added to game casseroles, and all have local names.

OIL

Spanish olive oil is usually "pure" – a mixture of virgin and refined oils. With its modest olive taste and comparatively high acidity, it is better for making mayonnaise than higher-priced and more famous virgin oils. In the 1970s much Spanish oil was exported to Italy – and re-labeled. Since the Arabs promoted its use in the kitchen, it has been used for frying and makes a surprisingly light and attractive sauce in liaison with a liquid. It is the healthiest of fats and is also the safest for deep frying.

Spanish virgin oil is easier to buy abroad than it is in Spain. The best is made at Baena, near Jaén, and around Lérida at Borjas Blancas, the Sierra de Segura and Siurana. It is very fruity – some taste almost appley.

Sunflowers, cut early when black, are also pressed to make a cheaper cooking oil, *aceite de girasol*.

ONION

Cebollas must be fried very slowly, to bring out their sweetness, quite different from their raw taste. Bigger than an orange, the yellow Spanish onion is the sweetest and mildest of all. A *sofrito* of slowly fried onion, with garlic, then tomato, added, is basic to many rice and soup recipes.

The oversize green onions or scallions, called *calçots* in Catalan and *cebollones* in Spanish, are good grilled (see page 65).

PACHARÁN

Spain's most popular generic liqueur, this dark, sweet, anise-flavored drink is made from sloes. It is drunk on the rocks and also makes a good fish sauce. Zoco is the best-known brand.

PAPRIKA AND CAYENNE

Pimentón fuerte, hot pepper, is cayenne, while *pimentón dulce* – called colored pepper, *pimentón colorado*, in the south – is paprika.

Paprika is an extremely important spice in the Spanish kitchen, used before frying, rather than as a cosmetic touch at the end. A little paprika will also help the balance of a dish, in the absence of traditional Spanish varieties of sweet and chili peppers, and eke out the more expensive saffron.

PINE NUTS

These tiny cream-colored nuts are extracted from the cones of stone pines, and are consequently expensive. The flavor is astringent, yet rich, much liked for sauces, vegetable dishes and expensive little cakes like *piñonates*.

RICE

One of the glories of Spanish cooking, Spanish rice is between a round and medium grain, and its unique characteristic is to absorb liquid without any stickiness (which is induced into other rices). Italian *risotto* rice was introduced by the Arabs to Italy at the same time, and is similar, though cooked very differently. Risotto rice is stirred regularly to encourage the rice to become sticky, but *paella* rice is washed to remove starch, then cooked without being stirred.

The rice should absorb the exact amount of liquid in which it is cooked, leaving it flavored, but each grain separate. Consequently, the quality of the stock is important. The rice will absorb double its own volume of liquid, or a little more, depending on the width of the pan, the heat source and the other ingredients. For four people you should allow 1 cup rice and 2 cups stock.

Indoors, cook rice over a heat diffuser, which spreads and diminishes the heat. Big pans are tricky: a thin or deep one is best cooked in the oven at 350°F after the last stir.

SAFFRON

Azafrán is an Arab spice, though it was introduced to Spain by the Romans, and Spain now produces the world's best saffron.

In La Mancha the saffron crocuses flower overnight and are picked around Santa Teresa's day in mid-October. The enormous expense of the spice reflects the fact that its three pistils must be plucked by hand from every flower. Nevertheless it is not a spice to economize on. Indeed, Nor-

man Douglas once said that, "A man who is stingy with saffron is capable of seducing his own grandmother."

A $\frac{1}{10}$ oz vial of Spanish saffron will include about 50 deep-red stamens, enough for an ordinary dish for 10 people or one dish *espléndido*. As the price of saffron has gone up, so the size of packages of saffron powder has gone down. They are now often $\frac{1}{25}$ oz, meaning three packages for a big dish. Cheap saffron, or any coming from a doubtful source, may be a dye or made of safflower, *cártamo*.

I have burned many expensive saffron strands trying to toast them on modern heat sources – they are just too hot! If you do need to toast saffron, however, papers of powder may be dry-fried until the paper colors. Before using, soak stamens for 20 minutes, and dissolve powder in 2 tablespoons of hot liquid.

SALCHICHÓN

A Spanish salami, *salchichón* is smooth and pink with specks of chopped fat and whole white peppercorns but no paprika. It makes a good *tapa* and stores well.

SALT AND PEPPER

The simpler the recipe, the more important is intelligent seasoning. Spain has good coarse salt, while that from Cadiz contains some saltpeter, which is good for hams and preserved sausages. The Catalans are generous users of black pepper, *pimienta*.

SHERRY

A mispronunciation of Jerez, sherry is a fortified wine from the southwest. In Spain dry sherry accompanies fish and *tapas*, but sherry's high alcohol content has made it on the whole a before- or after-dinner wine.

Sherries are blended in a *solera* system of stacked barrels, where new wine goes in the top and wine is then moved down to fill the lower tiers and drawn from the bottom. They are ranked for export in different sweetnesses, though in Spain each of them can vary quite widely within a given category. *Fino* is pale gold, crisp and dry, and *manzanilla* is the most delicate type of *fino*, influenced by the sea air of Sanlúcar, where it is stored. *Amontillado* is fuller-bodied, more golden and nuttier, and conventionally medium-

dry. *Palo cortado* comes in sweetness between this and *oloroso*, a mature, and usually sweeter, sherry.

The neighboring district of Montilla-Moriles produces very similar sherry-type wines which achieve the same alcoholic strengths without fortification, though some are in fact fortified. The pale dry Montilla is best known.

SOBRASADA

A soft, pâtélike sausage, largely of pork fat with some raw cured pork, it is flavored and colored with paprika. It may be served in pots for spreading on bread, or slices may go on top of large *ensaimada* breads. It is eaten in Mallorca and Catalonia.

SQUID AND CUTTLEFISH

When freshly caught their skins are pink, graying out of the water. Squid are mainly fried, or used in rice dishes or salads, but smaller ones, called *chipirones*, are stuffed.

Cuttlefish, called *jibia* or *sepia* – and *choco* if tiny – are stuffed or stewed.

They are prized for the black ink, in a bag inside them, that makes cleaning all of them a little tricky

STOCK

People curl up at the edges at the mention of fish stock. All I can say is: don't. First, it is very quick – unlike other stocks – taking 30 minutes at the outside. Second, the ingredients are not so difficult: look at shrimp stock on page 59, for example. All it needs is shrimp heads and vermouth.

The ingredients for the real thing – fish skin, bones and heads – can be bought in many street markets and supermarkets where fresh fish is sold. Get the messy work done for you by the fish man, but take the bits away with you. Then simmer with an onion, celery stalk, bay leaves, parsley stems and wine. Strain and add a strip of lemon zest to the hot stock.

Some supermarkets carry reduced fish stock and good fish soups. Canned clam juice and products like Clamato can also be used, while the Swiss make passable fish bouillon cubes.

If using cubes, remember two things. They should be used understrength with something else like vegetable water; a quarter of the quantity in wine is also a good rule. And never, ever use a cube and then reduce it. This will only expose the artificial base. Instead, look at the final amount of liquid and calculate the appropriate portion of cube.

Chicken stocks can be made from carcasses without legs, from butchers who sell breasts off the bone, and from chicken wings, and in Spain it is traditional to include a ham bone, which can be used several times. To remove any fat, draw strips of paper towel over the surface of the liquid.

SWEET PEPPERS

Spain has two types of sweet or bell pepper, only one of which is exported. The finest pepper in Spain is the *pimiento piquillo*, which is long and pointed: it means "beak-shaped." It is chiefly grown in Navarre and Rioja and it is distinctly hot. In Spain it's these thin-skinned peppers that are stuffed with salt cod or ground meat, made easier by their being sold ready in jars.

The fleshy, bell-shaped pepper, called *morrón*, "knobbly" pepper, in Spain, is extremely popular, though it is worth remembering that the green pepper is actually an underripe pepper of another color. Red peppers will always be sweeter and contain more vitamins. In Spain these are usually broiled or baked to remove the skin, after which the flesh may disintegrate to a sweet juice and a beautiful purée. These have a better flavor than canned red *pimientos*, which are much used as a convenient shortcut, because they are sold already skinned.

TOCINO

Salted pork fat – from the belly, not the back – *tocino* sometimes has rib bones in it and the block is cut to order. Rendered cubes of *tocino* are wonderful for frying onions.

Tocino is much more fatty than salt-cured pork sides, and recipes have been adjusted for this. The word is sometimes used for bacon.

TOMATOES

Really ripe tomatoes are used for sauce in Spain, lesser ones being relegated to salad. Ripe tomatoes are easy to peel; others may need 10 seconds in boiling water first. The flesh is then neatly cubed for salad, and dissolves easily to make a sauce. Add the leftover skin and seeds to stock, where they attract grease and scum, helping the stock to strain cleanly.

Outside Spain, canned tomatoes are often a redder, riper choice than fresh ones. A quick sauce is made from canned tomatoes added to *sofrito* (see ONION), then reduced and seasoned.

VINEGAR

Wine vinegar is used for vinaigrette and sauces. The vineyards of the south make sherry vinegar from young sherries that are reserved because of their high acidity. These are matured in wood and concentrated, so they are more intense than most wine vinegars.

WINE

Out to lunch on a special occasion, a Spanish family would probably choose a wine from either Rioja or Penedès, the two areas which took in French winemakers when the vineyards of the French were destroyed by phylloxera in the 19th century.

There is no longer a natural connection between regional food and wines in many areas, although Spain has more vineyards than any other country. Starting in the 19th century, and at an ever faster pace since the 1970s, the wines have been rethought with a ruthless commercial logic.

Spanish wines are blended wines. There are no restrictions on where the winemaker buys his grapes, or on the proportions in which he combines several types. The weather is hot and varies less than in other parts of Europe, too. So Spanish wines are sold on the winemakers' skill and the name on the bottle is like a brand name.

The white wines are unusually diverse. First there are those with a "sherry taste": dry, golden and very high in alcohol, like the white of Extremadura, the Chiclana of Cadiz and dry Montillas. Then there are the aristocratic, oak-aged whites, like Marqués de Murrieta, which have the virtues of their red counterparts. Rueda, home to the white Marqués de Murrieta, makes a fruity white from traditional grapes.

But many whites were thought to be insufficiently fruity or crisp and now wines are made in the French style, both in Penedès, where they are outstanding, and in Rioja. Fresh and fruity, wines like Rioja's Monopole are popular in Spain as well as in the export market for which they were designed. The main thing against them is that the taste often fades more quickly than in the French models.

There is also a small class of fresh "green" wines: the *alberiños* of Galicia, and white *chacolí* of which the Basques are so fond. *Cavas*, champagne-method sparklers, are popular and fine dessert wines are made from muscat grapes.

The young red wines make remarkably pleasant, easy drinking, being fresh and very fruity. Spaniards mostly drink *vino corriente*, which is labeled with the *cosecha*, harvest year, and is one or two years old. They are considerably less fussy about matching wine and food than other nations whose best wine is more highly esteemed.

The two main wine producing regions are La Mancha and the Levante coast, the latter producing undistinguished, high-alcohol reds. At the other end of the scale is Ribero de Duero, which produces Spain's undisputed best red, the almost-unobtainable Vega de Sicilia. In between, a number of drinkable reds come from places like Toro and Valdepeñas, while many Navarre wines have the virtues of the better-known Rioja.

Rioja is Spain's best-known wine

district, for it makes more complex wines that age well. Even so, less than half of its wine is wood-aged. The hallmark of Rioja is the whiff of vanilla that storage in oak casks gives to wine. New oak barrels make a wine taste strongly of vanilla. As the barrels are very expensive to replace, the winemakers move the wines around from barrel to barrel, sometimes four times in a year, to juggle each blend to best advantage. Minimum periods in the barrel are laid down for each class of wine. All white wines and *rosados*, rosés, must spend a minimum of 6 months in the barrel, while red wines must have a year, and *Gran reservas* a 2-year minimum. For the remaining time they mature in the bottle.

Think of the better barrel-aged wines like racehorses in three classes: 3-year-olds, 4-year-olds and 6-year-olds. The first are *crianzas*, the second *reservas*, the last *Gran reservas*. Simple math will tell you if a bottle is old for its class, and so may well have had longer

in the barrel than the minimum laid down. *Gran reservas* are wines spotted for their potential and given preferential treatment.

Some old-fashioned houses like Marques de Murrieta and Muga go for longer barrel-aging as part of their house style. Other modern *bodegas*, like Faustino Martínez and Olarra favor the minimum amount of oak and age in the bottle, a style that is popular in America.

Penedès is the other area of Spain known for large-scale production of quality wines. These differ from Rioja in two ways. Very few are barrel-aged. They are modeled on French wines and Torres, in particular, produces a dryer style of red than Rioja, which often includes French grapes, like Cabernet Sauvignon. The whites are fresh and fruity, experimenting with grapes like Chardonnay, and are more successful than attempts to do likewise in other parts of Spain. Also in the northeast, Raimat in Lérida produces successful wines from Cabernet Sauvignon.

TAPAS AND SOUPS

Tapas are nothing less than a way of life in Spain and the rich array of soups – from chilled summer refreshers to hearty winter warmers – bears witness to the geographical diversity of the country.

Left to right, from top PINCHITOS MORUNOS *(p 21)*, CHAMPIÑONES RELLENOS *(p 23)*, BUÑUELOS DE QUESO *(p 24)*, PELOTAS EN SALSA ROJA *(p 21)*, GAMBAS EN GABARDINAS *(p 26)*, MEJILLONES CON PIMIENTO VERDE Y ROJO *(p 26)*.

I CAN THINK OF NO PLACE where you can get such an extraordinary range of things to eat as in a *tapas* bar. The place promises drink and company, but the food is the lure to make you stay. Just as a Dubliner might go in search of ambience and whiskeys, so a Spaniard *va de pinchos*, goes looking for *pinchos*, delicious tidbits on skewers. A glorious selection is laid out on the bar, for the casual visitor to see, and to persuade him to linger.

The word *tapa* was originally used to mean a "cover," a piece of bread, balanced over a drink in a hostelry to keep out the flies in hot weather. Sausage or cheese would then be perched on top to make the bread appealing and, in days gone by, these were included in the price of the drink.

To lure and tempt you, a whole range of flavors is offered in tiny portions, from the sophisticated and exotic to the bland and soothing. Tasting and sharing them becomes a communal activity. The simplest *tapas* include some of Spain's best ready-to-eat food: scarlet raw *serrano* ham, black-waxed Manchego cheese, chunks of spicy *chorizo* sausage and, above all, marinated olives: *aceitunas aliñadas*. From the king-sized Obregóns, almost as plump as walnuts, conventional green *sevillanas extras*, to the small green *manzanillas* and the tiny grayish-brown *arbequines*, no bigger than fat Malaga raisins, everyone has a favorite. There are ripe ones, too, *negra dulce perlas*, or oily *aragonésas*.

There are also warming dishes available, of the best-loved nursery foods, for is this not a place of consolation, where men go after the trials of work? Simple, direct flavors can be savored in golden egg *tortilla, patatas bravas* – potatoes in a chili-hot tomato sauce – or chicken in garlic, and there is soothing food in familiar sauces, like kidneys with sherry and a variety of meatballs in tomato sauce.

In *tapas* bars Spaniards can indulge their passion for seafood. There are always shrimp on hand, then clams or mussels in white wine, marinated anchovies – and their backbones, fried to crunchy-crispness as a separate specialty – baby, stuffed squid, called *chipirones*, and the impenetrably dark potage of squid braised in its own ink.

Tapas will also be local dishes. In the Basque country you may find *angulas*, baby eels or elvers, of a gossamer thinness, tossed with hot chili oil in an earthenware bowl. Small, fried *kokotxas*, which are hake cheeks, are another specialty, and *gambas en gabardinas*, shrimp in a batter "raincoat," (see page 26) and pots of *txangurro*, or baked spider crab, may be found anywhere on the northern coast. Cadiz, in the southwest, is famous for its fried fish: like *acedías fritas*, baby soles, and *huevas*, crisp-fried fish roe. Shark, mostly dogfish, is appreciated stewed or battered. And, of course, there is the fried food that sums up Spain for the tourist, puffy rings of *calamares*, though in this corner of Spain squid are tiny ones, fried whole as *puntillitas*.

The idea behind *tapas* is that of a gap filler, an unwinder before the late dinner which is the habit in urban Spain. The food is also a prop for drinking, preventing one from becoming drunk, and, in origin at least, largely a male affair.

Many *tapas* make a good appetizer to a meal. The Spaniards also appreciate a dish all the more if it is an *entremés con apellido*, with a name or story attached to it. With these appetizers I have included soups, because of the way I thought the book would be used outside Spain. Spanish recipe books, however, group soups with pot meals and stews, and there is a very good reason for this. The pot of different meats, which are simmered together for the main course, also produces *caldo*, a beautiful broth, which is clear from very slow simmering. This is the basis of many soups, including the world-famous *consomé al Jerez*, which is more likely to be called *sopa viña A.B.* in Spain itself, from a sherry much favored for it.

There are a few well-known cream soups, like the salt cod *puré de Vigilia*, eaten during Lent, and bread is the base of another class of thin soup. Mule drivers, obviously a spoiled lot, have a bread and red wine version called *sopa de loro*, while everyone knows the chilled garlic-scented *gazpacho*.

Each province has its fish soups, often laced with alcohol against bad seaweather, like the mussel, tomato-and-*aguardiente sopa de mejillones* of the Catalans. The stew pot, full of fishy things, gives its name to another group, like the *caldeiradas* of Galicia (though in this book these fish soup-stews are included in Fish). In the countryside, however, the commonest of all soups are *potajes*: thick vegetable mixtures, full of this-and-that, like the cabbage-leaved *berzas*.

PELOTAS EN SALSA ROJA

TINY MEATBALLS
IN RED SHERRY SAUCE

There are quicker ways to make a tomato sauce, but this one is wonderfully simple. Its character depends on first-class pale dry *fino* sherry or Montilla wine.

SERVES 6 – 8

2 slices of stale bread
¼ cup lemon juice
1 lb ground pork or veal (or half and half)
¼ lb smoked uncooked ham, ground
⅓ cup finely chopped green olives
finely grated zest of ½ lemon
½ teaspoon coarse salt
pinch of cayenne
2 eggs, beaten, for coating
flour for coating
½ – ⅔ cup olive oil for frying

SALSA ROJA
1 onion, finely chopped
2 tablespoons olive oil
2 lb ripe tomatoes, without skin or seeds, or 28 oz
canned tomatoes, with juice
⅔ cup good fino *sherry or Montilla wine*

Start with the sauce. Fry the onion very slowly in the olive oil, letting it soften and darken. Add the tomatoes and simmer, stirring occasionally with a spoon, until the sauce is much reduced. (It's quicker to do this in two pans.)

Soak the bread in the lemon juice, then squeeze out lightly. Combine with all the other ingredients for the meatballs – this is easy in a food processor. Roll into balls the size of large marbles, then roll them in beaten egg. Shake them in a plastic bag containing flour, or to and fro on a floured plate, until lightly coated.

Heat the oil and fry the meatballs in one or two pans, shaking the pans to and fro every now and then, so they roll over and color evenly. When they are cooked, stir the *fino* into the sauce, pour over the meatballs and bring to a boil. Spear with toothpicks to serve.

PINCHITOS MORUNOS

SMALL SPICY MOORISH KABOBS

In Andalusia, every village store sells the spice mixture for these kabobs in a little box decorated with a red-turbaned Moor with a white beard. This is probably Spain's only ready-made spice mixture. It was pointed out to me that six of the ten spices in *pinchitos* are also in curry powder, and so a mild curry powder makes an excellent base to start from.

In Morocco the dish is made with lamb, but in Spain it is usually of pork, which has the big advantage that it can be marinated with salt. The first *pinchitos* I ever ate were slim strips of pork about 2 inches long, "stitched" with a small wooden skewer of about twice the length: more interesting than cubes which, of course, taste the same. Strips can be cut from pork veined with fat – shoulder butt, for example – following the natural grain.

SERVES 10 – 12

2 garlic cloves, finely chopped
2 teaspoons salt
1 teaspoon mild curry powder
1 teaspoon coriander seeds, ground
1 teaspoon paprika
¼ teaspoon dried thyme
plenty of freshly ground black pepper
3 tablespoons olive oil
1 tablespoon lemon juice
1 lb small pork cubes, or boneless pork shoulder butt,
cut into strips

Crush the garlic with the salt in a mortar, or with the flat of a knife on a board, then moving the paste to a bowl. Work in all the other marinating ingredients. Skewer the pork and turn the pieces (2 – 2½ dozen) in the marinade in a shallow dish, making sure that every one is coated all over. Leave to marinate over 2 hours and preferably longer.

Heat the broiler. Spread the *pinchitos* out well on the rack in the broiler pan and give them 2 – 3 minutes on each side, flipping them over with tongs.

POLLO AL AJILLO AL ESTILO DE PARELLADA

BONELESS GARLIC CHICKEN MORSELS

Chicken with garlic is one of the most typical Spanish dishes. It is generally the Spanish method to cut up birds with a chopper through the bone. This dish, however, is boneless, thanks to Juli Parellada, a 19th-century Barcelona dandy, who dared to ask for his *paella* "with all bones removed."

SERVES 6

2½-lb chicken
4 fat garlic cloves, finely chopped
2 teaspoons salt
about 5 tablespoons olive oil
freshly ground black pepper
1 tablespoon finely chopped parsley

Cut up the chicken, first slicing through the skin above the leg down to the joint, then working the knife toward the tail, making a downward scoop with the knife to pick up the "oyster" of meat on the backbone. Cut both legs free through the joint. Cut off both wings, working from the backbone (keep them to use for stock).

Reach into the neck and find the wishbone with your fingers; work along it and pull it out. Cut down on either side of the breastbone and work the breasts free. Peel off all the skin and cut the meat into bite-sized pieces. Halve the legs and take the meat off the bone in big pieces, discarding a bony plate over the chicken's knee. This will give you about ¾ pound of meat. Put this in a bowl.

Sprinkle the chopped garlic with the salt and mash with the flat of the knife to a paste (or use a mortar and pestle). Work in 1 tablespoon of olive oil. Season the chicken pieces with pepper and stir in the garlic paste. Leave to marinate until needed, stirring occasionally.

Heat 4 tablespoons of olive oil in a skillet and add the chicken pieces. Cook about 10 minutes over medium-high heat until golden, turning them over with a spatula. Put a sheet of paper towel in the bottom of the serving dish, and transfer the chicken. Remove the paper, sprinkle with a little parsley and serve with a jar of toothpicks on the plate.

TARTALETAS DE RIÑONES AL JEREZ

TARTLETS OF KIDNEYS IN SHERRY

On most *tapas* bars in Spain you will find kidneys in sherry sauce – pork kidneys in tomato sauce in the poorer south, more sophisticated veal or lamb kidneys in the cities – a warming *ración* to stave off the pangs of hunger. At home kidney sauce is served with rice or even pasta and may well include cubes of ham or bacon in a sauce thickened with flour and vegetables.

This elegant version, with a few spoonfuls of sherry sauce, is served in small tartlets suitable for a cocktail party. They should be eaten in two bites, so use small shallow tartlet molds, only $\frac{1}{4}$ inch deep, not the type sold for muffins or cupcakes.

SERVES 6 – 8

1 lb veal or lamb kidneys
2 tablespoons olive oil
2 tablespoons pork fat
1 garlic clove, finely chopped
$\frac{2}{3}$ cup fino *or* amontillado *sherry*
1 tablespoon tomato paste
2 tablespoons finely chopped parsley, plus extra to garnish (optional)

PASTRY

5 tablespoons unsalted butter, diced
$\frac{2}{3}$ cup flour, plus extra for rolling
$\frac{1}{4}$ cup coarse yellow cornmeal
$\frac{1}{4}$ teaspoon salt
about 2 tablespoons lemon juice

Make the pastry: cut the butter into the salted flour and cornmeal to make fine crumbs, then add enough lemon juice to make a smooth dough. Heat the oven to 350° F, and grease 16 tartlet molds. Roll out the pastry and cut out circles with a pastry cutter. Line the tartlet molds and bake about 8 minutes.

CAFÉ *The gentle click of dominoes is a typical sound in Spanish cafés, indispensable havens where people gather to eat and drink, discuss the world – or simply watch it go by.*

To prepare the kidneys, remove all membrane, cut out the middle core and then cut into large dice. Heat the oil and pork fat in a skillet and add the garlic. Over the highest heat put in the kidneys in handfuls, stirring them to seal cut surfaces. Pull them to the side and let the fat reheat before adding the next handful.

Add the sherry and stir the kidneys gently as it reduces to about 4 tablespoons. Stir in the tomato paste and parsley and remove from the heat. Spoon into the tartlet shells, sprinkle with a little more parsley if desired and serve immediately.

CHAMPIÑONES RELLENOS

STUFFED MUSHROOMS

Quick to make, this is one of the few hot *tapas* that can be easily cooked in the middle of a cocktail party. The recipe comes from Ana Diment Castillo at the Mesón Don Felipe in London. Hunt down your *chorizos* first, then buy button mushrooms of the right size to hold a slice of sausage when the stem is removed.

SERVES 8

about 1$\frac{1}{2}$ lb button mushrooms
salt
4 cooking chorizos or fresh spicy sausages
olive oil

Clean the mushrooms and remove the stems; salt the hollows lightly. Cut slices of *chorizo*, removing the skin, and push into the hollows. Brush the cap with oil, then place them cap side down on a baking sheet.

Heat the broiler. Broil the mushrooms 5 minutes until sizzling, and serve immediately.

BUÑUELOS DE QUESO

HOT FRIED CHEESE PUFFS

These puffs are much less interesting when they have been standing around – indeed *buñuelo* is slang for a "bungle" or "mess up" – so eat them almost immediately. To vary the batter, add 2 tablespoons of grated onion and a generous amount of cayenne to the cheese. Alternatively, try 4 tablespoons of chopped almonds or green olives with, or instead of, the cheese.

SERVES 6

3 tablespoons butter
¼ teaspoon salt
½ cup milk or water
½ cup flour, sifted
2 large eggs, beaten together
½ cup grated Manchego cheese, or Parmesan or Gruyère
½ teaspoon Dijon-style mustard
oil for deep frying
dusting of paprika or cayenne

Put the butter, salt and milk in a pan and bring slowly to a boil. Off the heat add the flour and beat hard with a wooden spoon. Return to the heat and beat until the mixture forms a ball around the spoon – 1–2 minutes. Remove from the heat again and add the beaten eggs, beating to a smooth paste. Stir in the grated cheese and the mustard.

Heat the oil in a deep fryer: to the top heat on an electric fryer, or until a bread cube will brown in 40 seconds. Using a teaspoon, and another to scrape it off, drop balls of the paste into the hot oil, 7–8 at a time. As soon as they pop to the surface, push them under with a slotted spoon, spinning them over. This helps them to color evenly and form a good round shape as they double in size. Cook about 5 minutes, until the outside is a dark gold and the inside is no longer pasty. Drain on paper towels.

Serve the *buñuelos*, dusted with paprika or cayenne, with toothpicks to pick them up. A nutty, medium-dry *amontillado* sherry is the ideal accompaniment.

BOQUERONES SIN TRABAJO

EFFORTLESS ANCHOVY SALAD

Black-backed fresh anchovies are caught all along the Mediterranean coast from Estepona on the Gibraltar road to Collioure over the French border. All they need is marinating and serving – hence the name – for a result totally unlike the canned fish.

SERVES 4

1 lb fresh anchovies, or sardines or smelts
about ¾ teaspoon salt
about ⅔ cup white wine vinegar
1 garlic clove, finely chopped
2 tablespoons chopped mild Spanish onion
3 tablespoons olive oil
2 teaspoons lemon juice
freshly ground black pepper
diced sweet red pepper and chopped parsley for garnish
(optional)

Cut off the heads and gut the fish, extending the cut beyond the stomach cavity as far as the tail. Turn each fish onto its belly and press your thumbs hard into the middle of the back: the fish will split open flat under pressure. Turn it over and pull out the backbone from the head end, snipping it free at the tail.

Lay the fish, skin side down, in a shallow dish and sprinkle with the salt, vinegar, garlic and onion. Leave in a cool place for 24 hours.

The following day, drain and rinse the fish (reserving some onion). Pat dry with paper towels. Dress the fish with a vinaigrette made from oil, lemon juice and seasonings, then sprinkle with a little marinated onion, plus sweet pepper and parsley for color. Serve with chilled *fino* sherry as a *tapa* for a group, or with salad for lunch for three to four people.

MEDICINAL HERBS *A market in Granada sells herbs to guard against a variety of ailments – a more unusual use than their customary culinary one.*

GAMBAS EN GABARDINAS

SHRIMP "IN RAINCOATS"

Protected from the heat of the oil by a crisp coating of batter, these shrimp are, literally translated, "wearing raincoats." It's the lightest and crispest fish batter that I know, and suitable only for ingredients that need little cooking. A pretty variation is to batter and fry a couple of strips of sweet red pepper and 3 large green olives per person, with fewer shrimp.

SERVES 4

1 lb large shrimp in the shell
olive oil for deep frying
1 lemon, cut into wedges

FRITTER BATTER
¾ cup flour
pinch of salt
3 tablespoons oil or melted butter
¾ cup lukewarm water
pinch of cayenne
1 egg white

Make the batter: put the flour and salt in a bowl, stir in the oil or butter and gradually work in the warm water to make a paste, then a smooth batter. Add a little cayenne. Let this stand while you peel the shrimp. Remove the heads and shells, but leave the tail tip.

Heat the deep-frying oil (to top heat on an electric fryer) until it will crisp a bread cube in 30–40 seconds. When the oil is hot, beat the egg white to soft peaks and fold it into the batter. Dip each shrimp into the batter, holding it by the tail, and then drop into the oil. Let the shrimp puff up and color for about 30 seconds, then remove with a slotted spoon to paper towels. Serve at once with the lemon wedges.

MEJILLONES CON PIMIENTO VERDE Y ROJO

COLD STUFFED MUSSELS WITH SWEET PEPPERS

The mussels of Galicia must be the best in the world – huge, sweet and bright orange like some strange fruit in a shell – and so tender they are eaten almost raw, just with lemon quarters. They are farmed in the western bays of the Atlantic coast, from little platforms with huts on top, that look like Chinese junks at sea.

In this simple recipe the mussels are gently steamed, then served with a crisp dice of red and green sweet peppers, which adds color and a new texture, making this a very attractive *tapa*.

Double the amounts given in the recipe for an appetizer for four people and double them again for a cocktail party for 24, when people will probably only eat a couple of mussels each.

SERVES 4

½ cup dry white wine
salt and freshly ground black pepper
1 lb large mussels, cleaned (see page 96)
1–2 teaspoons lemon juice
¼ sweet green pepper
¼ sweet red pepper

Heat the wine in a saucepan with a grinding of pepper, and put in a handful of mussels at a time. Steam them, covered, 2–3 minutes. When open, fish them out and start removing top shells. Discard any that don't smell sweet or remain closed. Arrange the halves, 2 mussels in each shell, on a serving plate.

To remove any sand, strain the juices into a smaller pan through cheesecloth inside a strainer (or a coffee filter). Then boil to reduce to about 4 tablespoons of concentrated juice. Taste and season very carefully, adding a little lemon juice at a time, and salt and pepper if needed.

Use a coffee spoon to dribble a little juice over each mussel, just to glaze them. Dice the sweet peppers very finely and sprinkle both colors in each shell. Chill until needed, but serve the same day.

A chilled white wine from Ribeiro is a natural

partner for this simple dish. This "green" Albariño wine is flowery and somewhat acid: one of Spain's best fish wines. It is usually slightly sparkling, in the style of *vinho verde* from Portugal, which is made from the same grapes, just over the border. However, the Spanish wines will seem dryer, as the Portuguese wines are sweetened for export. Best known is Palacio de Fefiñanes, which is not sparkling.

CHANQUETES

DEEP-FRIED WHITEBAIT

Tiny, transparent fish called *chanquetes* swim, sometimes in huge banks, off the southern coast of Spain – the *fideos* or thin spaghetti of the sea. Such fish, as well as others like baby anchovies and sardines, are deep-fried – an art at which Spaniards excel. Although they are often fried in batter (see page 26), flour makes the better coating for fish as thick as whitebait, the fry of fish such as herring and silverside – our closest equivalent to *chanquetes*.

SERVES 4

1 lb very fresh whitebait
olive oil for deep frying
¼ cup flour
½ teaspoon salt
freshly ground black pepper
dusting of cayenne
wedges of lemon to serve

Rinse the fish and pat dry with plenty of paper towels. Heat enough oil for deep frying to 375° F – top temperature on an electric fryer and just below smoking point for olive oil. A bread cube should crisp in 30–40 seconds.

Put the flour and seasonings in a plastic bag and add a handful of fish. Shake to coat them, then remove the fish to a plate; this minimizes the amount of flour that goes into the fryer. Add the fish to the hot oil and fry 1½–2 minutes until lightly golden. Faint blisters will appear on the sides of the fish. Remove with a slotted spoon to paper towels to drain.

Only coat the second batch while the first fish are frying, so the flour has no chance of becoming wet. Fry all the fish, in 5–6 batches, draining each batch on clean paper towels. Sprinkle with cayenne and serve immediately with lemon wedges to squeeze over them.

Strain the oil immediately after use, then heat a long strip of lemon zest in it to remove the fishy smell. Even after this, keep the oil for fish only.

GAMBAS PIL-PIL

SIZZLING CHILI-HOT SHRIMP

These shrimp are immensely popular, not least because this is a good way of disguising previously cooked, and even frozen, shrimp. The recipe below is for serving with cocktails, but the dish is often made as an appetizer, in individual dishes. Small *cazuelitas* are heated in the oven and each person is then given at least 4–5 tablespoons of oil with the shrimp. Heavily flavored with chili peppers, the oil is a popular part of the dish. The little pots are carried to the table, each covered by a piece of bread to stop the oil spitting, and the bread then serves to mop up the oil.

SERVES 4

2 garlic cloves
6–7 tablespoons olive oil
2 small dried chili peppers or 1 fresh one, stem and
seeds removed, or ¼–1 teaspoon chili powder
½–¾ lb peeled large shrimp, thawed if frozen
pinch of paprika

Crush the garlic cloves with the flat of a knife. Heat the oil in a skillet with the garlic and sliced fresh chili pepper, if using, or dried chili pepper or powder. When the garlic browns, discard it and the dried chili pepper; a fresh one should remain in the pan.

Blot the shrimp well with paper towels if they are thawed, toss in very hot oil for a minute or so until opaque and sprinkle with paprika. Serve in a very hot dish with the oil and fresh chili pepper and eat with toothpicks.

MANTECA COLORADA

PAPRIKA PORK RILLETTES

This is a good help-yourself appetizer for a group of people sitting together, with a bottle of wine, watching the sun go down and lazily waiting for dinner. Textured with little shreds of pork, the soft red pork fat is rather similar to the *sobrasada* sausage, sold in and out of its skin, so popular in Mallorca.

SERVES 8

14 oz pork fatback without rind
14 oz fresh porksides
3 fat garlic cloves
6 tablespoons fino *sherry*
2 bay leaves, crumbled
2 tablespoons paprika
plenty of freshly grated nutmeg
1 teaspoon salt
plenty of freshly ground black pepper

Heat the oven to 275° F. Cube the fat as small as you can. Cut the pork sides into rectangles following the grain of the meat, so that there will be 1-inch shreds of pork later. Put the meat and fat cubes into a casserole warming on the stove. Crush the garlic cloves with the flat side of a knife and add to the casserole with the sherry.

Move the covered casserole to the oven for 1 hour, then stir and season well with the herbs and spices. Stir again, then cook very gently about 5 hours (this is a good partner in the oven for meringues).

Turn into a colander over a heatproof bowl. Press the fat with the back of a spoon, then pick the meat cubes to pieces with two forks, adding the shredded meat to the liquid fat in the bowl. Discard what is left of the cubes. Taste the liquid fat to check the seasonings. In Spain this is packed into the same tall, straight-sided brown terra-cotta pots that are used for yogurt. It makes about 1 pint. Chill until needed, then serve with French bread.

PA AMB TOMÀQUET CON JAMÓN Y QUESO

TOMATO BREAD WITH RAW HAM AND CHEESE

In Catalonia bread is rarely put on the table without an accompanying tomato. When the summers are hot – and the tomatoes therefore superior – I eat Catalan tomato bread for lunch almost every day, for it makes the ideal foil to salad. It's both delicious and economical – a similar idea to the *chaponnade* of garlic bread in the bottom of a Provençal salad bowl. Here it's topped with Spain's best raw ham and cheese.

SERVES 8

1 long French loaf
about ½ lb jamón serrano *or* prosciutto, *sliced thinly*
about 10 oz Manchego cheese or young Parmesan, sliced thinly
1½ lb ripe red tomatoes
6 – 8 garlic cloves
pitcher containing ½ cup olive oil

Slice the French bread diagonally and cut the ham and cheese into pieces no larger than the bread. Arrange on two plates. Put everything on the table together with side plates and knives. Toast the bread very lightly.

To eat, each person cuts a tomato in half and squeezes the tomato juice onto each side of the toast. Next, halve the garlic cloves and wipe the cut side onto the juice. Finally, sprinkle a teaspoon or so of olive oil on top. *Aficionados*, especially in the Val d'Arran in the Pyrenees, will eat it just like this, but the more sophisticated version is to top the toasts with a slice each of raw ham and cheese.

SQUARE IN LÉRIDA *The morning's shopping is interrupted by a chat in the town square, invariably the hub around which Spanish towns and villages revolve.*

OLIVE TREES IN ANDALUSIA (overleaf) *Seemingly endless olive groves stretch as far as the eye can see – a typical landscape in Andalusia, whose parched, arid land is particularly suited to olive-growing.*

GAZPACHO ROJO DE SEVILLA

SEVILLIAN CHILLED RED SOUP

Gazpacho dates back to before Roman times, in origin a primitive soup with the chill of cold stone floors and icy well water. Foreigners looked down on it as a provincial dish – *caspa* is Italian for "remains" or "bits," *acho* is derogatory. Fame came in the 19th century, after sweet peppers, cucumbers and tomatoes were added.

Spaniards say there are "as many different *gazpachos* as there are mortars and pestles" and how a cook prepares a *gazpacho* betrays his or her regional origin. The Madrid version includes mayonnaise, and others may include morsels of game and stock. In winter it is a hot soup, even a thick one. But it is at its best and most refreshing served chilled, in hot weather.

SERVES 6

2 slices white bread, without crusts
1 small onion, roughly chopped
2 garlic cloves, finely chopped
pinch of cayenne
2 tablespoons olive oil
1 teaspoon coarse salt
*1 English cucumber, half the skin and all the
seeds removed*
*½ lb sweet red pepper (green if using tomato juice),
without stem or seeds*
2 tablespoons sherry vinegar or red wine vinegar
*1 lb ripe red tomatoes, without skin or seeds, or 16 oz
canned tomatoes and juice, or 3 cups tomato juice
(omitting half the ice water later)*
3½ cups ice water

GARNISH
a selection from the following:
¼ cup freshly fried croutons
¼ cup chopped sweet pepper, red or green
2 hard-cooked eggs, peeled and chopped
*¼ cup chopped mild Spanish onion
or scallions*
a handful of green or ripe olives, pitted and chopped

AJO BLANCO CON UVAS DE MÁLAGA *top,* GAZPACHO
ROJO DE SEVILLA *bottom.*

Cover the bread with water, then squeeze it out. Put the bread, onion, garlic and cayenne in a blender with the oil and salt and purée everything. Add the cucumber, sweet pepper, vinegar and the tomato or juice. You will probably have to make it in two batches.

Chill at least 12 hours, preferably overnight, turning the refrigerator down to its lowest setting, or put it in the freezer for about 30 minutes.

Before serving, dilute with ice water – but, preferably, don't serve with ice cubes in it. Arrange the garnishes in little dishes and pass them around on a tray.

AJO BLANCO CON UVAS DE MÁLAGA

CHILLED ALMOND SOUP, MALAGA-STYLE, WITH GRAPES

White *gazpacho* goes back at least 1,000 years, to the time when Moors ruled much of Spain. It was originally made by pounding almonds with icy well water and was particularly soothing in the heat of the Andalusian summer. This is the more sophisticated, creamy *Malagueñan* version, with a sweet grape garnish.

SERVES 4 – 5

½ lb white stale bread or rolls, without crusts
2 garlic cloves, peeled
pinch of salt
2 – 3 tablespoons olive oil
2 tablespoons sherry vinegar or white wine vinegar
1½ cups freshly ground almonds
2½ cups ice water
½ lb white grapes, seeded

Pour water over the bread, then squeeze it out. Tear into pieces and put them in a blender with the garlic cloves. Add the salt and olive oil, and purée everything.

Add the vinegar and almonds with enough ice water to blend until smooth. Slowly add the remaining water with the blender running, to make a cream. Chill at least 2 hours. Check the seasonings, ladle into bowls and garnish with grapes.

SOPA DE AJO CON HUEVOS

GARLIC SOUP
WITH POACHED EGGS

All over Spain people eat garlic soups – from the humble varieties, like beggars' soup in Avila, made only from fried garlic and bread crumbs, colored with paprika and diluted with saltwater, to richer ones – like the soup of "bread, garlic, paprika and beaten egg," which Alexandre Dumas thought worth recording on his journey through Castile in the 1840s. In La Mancha, a similar soup is served to lovers on their wedding night, to "raise their morale."

SERVES 4

2 thick slices of country-style (not soft-textured)
bread, without crusts
2 tablespoons olive oil
4 garlic cloves, finely chopped
1 teaspoon paprika
3½ cups light stock or water
salt
4 eggs

Heat the oven to 325° F with 4 individual casseroles or ovenproof soup plates. Fry the bread in oil in a flameproof casserole, with the garlic in one corner, making sure it doesn't burn. After turning the bread, sprinkle the top with paprika. Remove the bread and garlic to a blender and purée with a little stock or water. Return to the casserole and add the remaining stock or water – adding more salt if water alone is used. Bring to a boil.

Break the eggs into the soup plates and ladle in the soup. Bake them in the oven about 8 minutes to allow the eggs to set slightly. If you don't want to heat the oven just for this, the eggs can be beaten into the hot soup.

BAKER'S SHOP IN CASTILE *Panadería points to a bakery in this somewhat unlikely setting. No Spanish table would be complete without crusty, freshly baked bread to accompany the meal and Castile, where conditions are perfect for wheat-growing, is said to produce Spain's finest bread.*

SOPA DE PICADILLO

CLEAR SOUP WITH HAM,
EGG AND MINT

I like the clear fresh taste of mint and ham in this soup. *Picadillo* usually means ground meat, but ham is the traditional garnish for this soup, which is made from *caldo de puchero*, broth from the stockpot. In former times, this broth was a standard item, at least in meat-eating households, for meats were boiled at least once a week for dishes like *cocido madrileño* (see page 104). And very good it is too, with no vegetable flavors, just distilled meat essences. Famous soups, like *consomé al Jerez*, sherried consommé, are based on it. Bad broths, of course, exist. Richard Ford clearly ate one in the 1840s, when he commented that the stockpot, or "*olla*, is made of 2 cigars boiled in 3 gallons of water."

I use chicken stock made with carcasses, but try to include a ham hock, often its second cooking, and some chickpeas (*garbanzos*) when making it.

SERVES 4

1 quart light meat or chicken stock
¼ lb raw or smoked ham, cubed
salt and pepper
leaves from 4 sprigs of mint
2 hard-cooked eggs, chopped

Heat the stock with the chopped ham. Check the seasoning, add the mint and chopped egg and serve.

PURRUSALDA

LEEK AND POTATO SOUP

The name of this soup comes from leeks, *puerros*, and *saldo* – meaning "well-balanced" and also the name of a local Basque dance. Sometimes the soup contains *bacalao*, or salt cod. This is soaked and briefly fried, and the soup is then made with water, rather than stock.

SERVES 6

*4 leeks, keeping a little of the green tops (about
1 lb after trimming)
2 tablespoons pork or chicken fat, or butter
1 lb potatoes, sliced very thinly, then quartered if large
2 garlic cloves, finely chopped
salt and white pepper
2¼ cups meat or chicken stock
toast to serve*

The easiest way to clean leeks is to split them half through lengthwise, then turn them upside down in a pitcher of cold water. After 10 minutes, drain and cut them into rings.

Sweat the leeks in hot fat until they collapse. Add the potatoes and garlic, season with salt and pepper, and fry for a moment, stirring gently. Pour in the stock and cook 15–20 minutes. Check the seasoning and serve with bread toasted in the oven.

Soup made with meat stock is best eaten freshly made and is sometimes served with a crust of grilled cheese on top. A cream soup can be made if you use chicken stock: increase the amount of liquid slightly and then purée it.

PURRUSALDA

CALDO GALLEGO

GALICIAN CABBAGE SOUP

A warming soup for the cold, opening months of the year, *caldo gallego* also has a spring freshness. It is so popular outside Galicia that all the items for it are sold especially in Madrid. Traditionally it's made with *grelos*, the top spring leaves of turnips, with the buds just coming into flower, though the side shoots of cabbage are used instead in the Basque country. The new potatoes are special too – called *cachelos*.

The other constituent is salted meat. The old way of the farmer's wife was to use an *unto* – a ham bone aged for at least 5 years, with a little *tocino*. Sometimes translated as "bacon," this word embraces the salt-cured ribs of pork sides and a great deal of fat. I've used fresh spare ribs successfully; or use salted pork sides, whichever is easiest.

SERVES 6

1⅓ cups dried Great Northern or other white beans
¾ lb pork spare ribs or ¼ lb salt pork
1 lb smoked ham hock with a little meat attached
1 lb potatoes, egg-sized, halved
½ lb tender turnip greens, collards, chard or kale
salt and freshly ground black pepper

Pour boiling water over the beans and let soak an hour. If using spare ribs, rub them well with salt. If using salt pork, put it into a pan with the ham hock, cover with cold water and bring to the boiling point. Simmer 5 minutes, then drain. Cube the salt pork.

Put the ham hock, spare ribs or cubed salt pork and drained beans into a flameproof casserole and cover with 2 quarts water. Bring to the simmering point, skim off any scum, then cook gently, covered, 1 hour.

Add the halved potatoes and simmer another 20 minutes. Prepare the greens, removing thicker stems. Remove all the bones from the pot and check the stock for salt and pepper. Add the greens to the pot and simmer another 5 – 10 minutes. Meanwhile, remove all the edible meat from the bones and return it to the pot. To thicken the liquid a little, fish out a few potatoes, mash and return them.

CALDILLO DE PERRO

CADIZ FISH SOUP WITH ORANGE

The affection in which this winter soup is held is indicated by the diminutive "little soup." *Perro* means "dog" and the soup comes from the fishermen's quarters at Puerto de Santa Maria, which commands the incomparable Cadiz harbor. There is also a "cat" soup – though perversely it is fishless.

SERVES 6

2 lb young hake or whiting, probably 3 fish, filleted,
with the heads, bones and belly trimmings
2 teaspoons salt
juice of 4 Seville oranges or 3 sweet ones
5 garlic cloves
2 tablespoons olive oil
1 large onion, finely chopped
juice of 2 lemons (if using sweet oranges)
freshly ground black pepper
1 orange, peeled, sliced and quartered

Cut the hake fillets into slices 3-inches long and sprinkle the cut side with the salt. The flesh of immature hake is very soft and pink (unlike mature fish) and salt stiffens it. The belly cavity is unusual in being lined with a thick black skin and the quickest way to fillet (especially for soup) is to confine the fillets to the upper sides and backs of the fish.

Put the heads, bones and belly trimmings into a saucepan and add 5 cups water and a spiral of zest from one orange. Bring to the simmering point, skim, then simmer, covered, 30 minutes.

Crush the garlic cloves with the flat of a knife. Heat the oil in a soup pot over high heat and add the garlic. When the cloves color, discard them and turn down the heat. Fry the onion gently until softened, then strain in the hot fish stock and bring back to a boil.

Add the hake pieces, a few at a time, without letting the soup go off the boil. Cook 15 – 20 minutes, add the juice from the oranges (and lemon) and check the seasoning. Garnish with quartered orange slices.

SHEEP IN GALICIA *The black sheep lives up to its reputation and strikes out alone in the lush green countryside of Galicia.*

EGGS, RICE
AND PASTA

*The simple, delicious staples of eggs and rice
are indispensable to the country food of
Spain, and the more modern pasta has
introduced a new note into traditional
cooking.*

PAELLA VALENCIANA *(p53)*.

EGGS ARE THE FOOD OF country folk – as in Ireland, in earlier times in Spain much was measured by the value of an egg. Egg dishes are still very much a basic part of Spanish cuisine, listed as a separate course on the menu. These are country dishes, making good use of small amounts of food, gathered fresh that morning from the garden plot, when the hen's egg was also retrieved warm from the place where she hid it.

Rice is treated in the same way, flavored by small additions of vegetables, pork or seafood. It has been part of the Spanish diet since the Arabs introduced it to Valencia in the 9th century, on land the Romans had irrigated. It's a basic food in the south, stuffed into vegetables, accompanying stews and forming the base of salads. The Catalans bake it as *arròs passejat*, meaning "walked rice," for in the past it went out of the house to be cooked in the baker's oven. The north of Spain, however, accepted rice first as a milk pudding.

Spain's most famous rice dish, *paella*, is firmly based in Valencia on the east coast and is probably only two centuries old. It comes from La Huerta, meaning "the market garden," near Lake Albufera to the south of the city. This is one of the largest freshwater lakes in Spain and the home of delicious eels. So the original *paella* may well have been a Lenten mixture of eels, snails and vegetables like *garrafones*, the local white beans. It was cooked out-of-doors over a fire of vine prunings and *paella* is still the most enchanting of outdoor foods. The saffron-gold of the rice is flecked with red, green and pink and the different shapes of shellfish, and each of the small surprises it contains has a new flavor and texture.

Paella is traditionally a dish cooked by men – outside, as barbecues are – with preparations shared pleasantly over a bottle of wine. A group of people, though, means the shallow pan must be a big one – 15 inches across and sometimes more. Such pans need low heat, ideally as wide as the pan, and out-of-doors hot charcoal can be spread out to provide this. This is not so easy to manage indoors, though a heat diffuser works well.

Big *paellas* are often cooked in the oven from the point when all the stock is included and they have been stirred for the last time. However, this rules out one of the charms of a garden *paella*: the *socarrat*, a toasted golden crust at the bottom of the pan. The best *paella* pans have a dimpled bottom to prevent this sticking.

To outsiders, Valencian *paella* is known for its chicken and seafood mixture, but this famous dish has many local versions. *Arròs en perdiu*, rice with "partridge," is a Lenten dish from the same province. It includes chickpeas with the rice and, as meat was forbidden during Lent, the bird of the title is in fact a whole bulb of garlic.

Paellas are cooked until all the liquid has been absorbed by the rice, when the rice becomes "dry." But the Valencia area also has soupy rice dishes, *arroces caldosos*, which are cooked in the *caldero* pot like many famous fish stews on both the north and east coasts. Very often these are fishy rice stews, bolstered with vegetables and a little *ñora* chili pepper, which is popular on the Alicante coast. Beans and turnips are the backbone of the Valencian *arròs amb fesols i naps*, but this also includes pork in the form of pig's ears, a foot and blood sausage, and is cooked in the traditional *olla*.

Paellas can absorb everything the countryside has to offer: frog and rabbit, game birds and chicken have all become constituents of *paella*. There are game *paellas* and, more modestly, vegetable ones, though almost all of them are usually flavored with various parts and products of the pig.

The best-loved *paellas*, however, are those containing seafood, and there is a natural affinity between them and fish. The key to a *paella*'s success is a splendid stock. It is both aesthetic and practical, therefore, to start with fish stock, since fish produces so much debris that cannot be used in any other way than for soup.

The introduction of pasta to Spain has given rise to what appears to be a new *paella* seafood dish, the *fideuà*, in which pasta has replaced the traditional rice. Pasta has become popular generally and a big factory in Malaga produces it for the south and east. It is cooked in two main ways. *Fideos*, a very short spaghetti, comes in various thicknesses that go into soups. Like the rest of us, the Spaniards also make macaroni and cheese. A great influx of Italian chefs in the 19th century spread ideas such as cheese sauce and introduced *canelones* to Spain. Cannelloni is now a popular dish, eaten on Saint Stephen's Day (the day after Christmas), though the cannelloni tube is still not on sale. The local version is half-sheets of lasagne, bought in packages, then cooked and rolled at home.

TORTILLA ESPAÑOLA

SPANISH POTATO OMELET

Invented by a peasant for a hungry king, so the story goes, the *tortilla* has been made for at least 400 years – a dense moist cake of egg, totally different from the French omelet. *Tortillas* with potato have been a favorite since the 18th century, but they can contain anything you fancy. In the following recipe the potato could be replaced by ½ pound onions, softened until golden, or fat shrimp, or spoonfuls of *samfaina* (see page 89).

There are only two rules. The first is that the contents must not greatly exceed the volume of eggs, and the second is that the additions must not drip – either with sauce or with oil. Serve *tortillas* hot, warm or cold. This recipe will make an appetizer for four people or supper for two.

SERVES 4

about ½ cup olive oil
1 lb potatoes, peeled and diced
6 extra-large eggs
salt and freshly ground black pepper

Don't use too large a skillet – one about 9 inches across with sides is needed to produce a sponge-cake shape with vertical sides. Heat a generous quantity of oil until very hot, add the potatoes and stir them so they are coated with oil. Reduce the heat and let the potatoes cook through, turning them over frequently so they do not color.

Use a slotted spoon to move the potatoes to a bowl with a layer of paper towel at the bottom. Drain the oil from the skillet into a cup and wipe out the pan with paper towel if there are any sticky or crusty patches.

Strain about 2 tablespoons of oil back into the skillet, and reheat. Beat the eggs together and season them well. Pull the paper from under the potatoes and pour the eggs over them, so they are well coated. Pour the mixture into the hot oil, spreading the potatoes evenly, and give it a minute at high heat to set, before turning down the heat. Use a spatula to pull the *tortilla* off the sides of the skillet to make an upright edge, shaking the pan to and fro occasionally, to make sure the bottom isn't sticking.

WROUGHT-IRON GRILLES *In former times, the grilles on these houses in Andalusia protected the daughter of the house sitting within from the attentions of her admirer, wooing her from the other side.*

When the top has ceased to be liquid, cover with a serving plate and reverse the skillet to turn the *tortilla* out. Add 2 more tablespoons of oil, return the *tortilla* to the skillet – cooked side up – and cook a further 2–3 minutes. Serve hot, alone or with tomato sauce or *samfaina* (see page 89).

Some people like it even better cold – in a thick wedge with a salad of tomato and mint, or cut into cubes and served as a *tapa* on a stick. Traditionally, poor farm workers took a chunk of *tortilla*, sandwiched in a *bocadillo*, to the fields for their midday meal. Once cooked, a *tortilla* will keep for a couple of days and even reheats well in tomato sauce.

PIPERRADA VASCA

BASQUE SWEET PEPPER OMELET

There are many chopped vegetable sauces in the Spanish repertoire, but this one has a creamy French sophistication – not surprising since it comes from the Basque country, half of which is in France. The texture is achieved by charring and skinning the peppers beforehand, so they are soft enough to melt into the eggs. The cold mixture also makes a very good filling for a *bocadillo* sandwich.

SERVES 4

1 lb sweet peppers, red or green
¼ cup oil
1 onion, chopped
1 garlic clove, finely chopped
1 lb ripe tomatoes, without skin or seeds, or 16 oz canned tomatoes, drained
6 extra-large eggs
salt and freshly ground black pepper
4 slices of ham or Canadian bacon

Broil the peppers whole for about 20 minutes, giving them a quarter turn every 5 minutes, until they are charred on all sides. Transfer them to a plastic bag for 10 minutes.

Meanwhile, heat 2 tablespoons of oil in a skillet and cook the onion slowly until golden, adding the garlic near the end. Chop the tomato flesh (or pulse briefly in a processor) and add to the pan. Remove the skin from the peppers, discarding stems and seeds, and chop (or process briefly). Add to the pan and cook to a soft sauce.

Beat the eggs together, season and pour over the vegetables, stirring them together to make a soft, creamy, orange-colored mixture, then fry like a French omelet without stirring. Fry the ham or bacon in 2 tablespoons of oil and serve together.

CHORICERO CHILI PEPPERS *In this Rioja village a brazier is used to char peppers, prior to skinning them. Hanging out to dry on the wall behind are glorious red bundles of sweet chili peppers,* choriceros, *which give their color, taste and name to* chorizo *sausages.*

REVUELTO DE ESPÁRRAGOS TRIGUEROS

SCRAMBLED EGGS WITH YOUNG ASPARAGUS

"Everyone who has visited southern Spain in the spring," says Gerald Brenan in *South from Granada*, "will have sampled the thin, bitter asparagus. This is never planted in gardens, but is picked from a tall thorny plant that grows on every mountain slope in southern Spain that is not too far from the sea." I have never picked it myself, but in April I have met people with bundles of *trigueros* under their arms while I was hunting for bee-orchids, which share the same season. Since then the two have always been pleasantly connected in my mind.

Revuelto means "stirred," but "soft-set" is a better description of these eggs. The Spaniards scramble eggs in a skillet and make the distinction between eggs that are stirred while cooking, which remain soft underneath, and *tortillas*, which set to a golden crust (see page 43).

SERVES 4

¾ lb thin green asparagus
2 tablespoons butter
8 extra-large eggs
2 tablespoons milk
2 tablespoons olive oil
salt and freshly ground black pepper

Scrape the asparagus from below the bud to the base, removing points and the stringy outside of the stems. Cook in boiling water in a wide casserole (or in a roasting pan on top of the stove if they are long) until almost soft. This will take 8 – 10 minutes for cultivated asparagus; wild asparagus is hard and bitter and needs 30 minutes and a change of water.

Drain the asparagus and cut into 1½-inch lengths, discarding tough ends. Heat the butter in two skillets until frothing, then turn the asparagus in the hot fat. Beat the rest of the ingredients together and pour in. Turn up to medium-high heat and scramble the eggs lightly, stirring the outside to the middle with a wooden spoon. Serve this lovely creamy spring dish with crusty bread.

REVUELTO CON SETAS

SCRAMBLED EGGS WITH WILD MUSHROOMS

The better the quality of the mushrooms in this dish, the less egg is used – just enough to bind them together when wild mushrooms are in season. If button mushrooms are substituted, use an extra egg. The dish is best made in a non-stick pan.

SERVES 2

2 tablespoons butter
1 tablespoon olive oil
1 garlic clove, finely chopped
½ lb oyster or fresh shiitake *mushrooms*
3 extra-large eggs
1 tablespoon milk
salt and freshly ground black pepper
1 tablespoon finely chopped parsley

Heat the butter and oil in a skillet until foaming. Add the garlic and the sliced mushrooms and cook over medium heat, turning occasionally with a wooden spoon, until they are soft. If they give off juice, turn up the heat and boil it away.

Beat the eggs with the milk, seasoning and parsley, and add to the pan. Cook over medium heat, pulling the eggs to the middle until just set. Serve at once.

HUEVOS A LA FLAMENCA

COLORFUL BAKED EGGS

With its swirl of red, green, yellow and white, this dish has all the vibrant color of the whirling skirts of gypsy dancers. Shrimp can be substituted for the sausage, or everything included in a grand medley.

SERVES 4

¼ cup olive oil
1 large onion, chopped
2 garlic cloves, finely chopped
¼ lb cooking chorizo *or fresh spicy sausage, sliced, or* smoked ham, *cubed*
2 sweet red or green peppers (⅓ lb), chopped
¾ lb ripe tomatoes, without skin or seeds, or 1½ cups canned tomatoes, with juice
1 – 2 tablespoons fino *or* amontillado *sherry*
¾ cup shelled peas
¼ lb green beans, snapped in short lengths
8 extra-large eggs
pinch of cayenne
salt

Heat the oven to 350° F and warm a shallow casserole or baking dish.

Heat the oil in a skillet and soften the onion slowly. Add the garlic and push to the sides of the pan, then fry the sausage or ham until colored and remove it. Add the sweet peppers and chopped tomato to the pan and let them cook and reduce, stirring occasionally. Add some sherry if the mixture seems dry. Meanwhile, cook the peas and beans and add them too.

Transfer the vegetable mixture to the casserole and distribute the sausage or ham. Swirl the eggs together with a fork without overmixing, seasoning them well with cayenne and salt. Pour over the vegetables and meat and bake in the oven about 10 – 15 minutes until the eggs are just set.

HUEVOS A LA FLAMENCA

CHALK SOIL IN GRANADA (overleaf) *The lime-green shades in this starkly impressive Andalusian landscape indicate chalky soil, which, further west in Jerez, produces ideal conditions for the cultivation of sherry grapes.*

PISTO MANCHEGO CON HUEVOS FRITOS

TOMATO STEW WITH DEEP-FRIED EGGS

A pleasant appetizer from La Mancha, Don Quixote country in central Spain, which makes a good supper dish. Use pumpkin toward the end of the year and zucchini, or ½ pound green beans, in summer. Beans will need 3–4 tablespoons of stock too, as they take up moisture rather than adding it.

Deep-fried eggs will be a surprise to anyone who has not eaten them – they are deliciously light, puffy and digestible. It's worth making double the amount of *pisto*, if you have time, for it is an excellent sauce to serve with poultry or for reheating rice.

SERVES 3 – 4

2 tablespoons oil
2 onions (about ½ lb), chopped
¼ lb smoked Canadian bacon, in strips
2 garlic cloves, finely chopped
2 sweet green peppers (about ½ lb), seeded and chopped
1 lb ripe tomatoes, without skin or seeds, or 16 oz canned tomatoes, with juice
¾ lb cubed zucchini (unpeeled) or pumpkin
salt and freshly ground black pepper
pinch of freshly ground nutmeg
olive oil for deep frying eggs
1 – 2 eggs per person
1 – 2 tablespoons finely chopped parsley

Heat the oil in a skillet or flameproof casserole and soften the onion with the bacon, adding the garlic toward the end. Add the sweet peppers and fry 5 minutes. Add the tomatoes with their juice, and the zucchini or pumpkin and cook over low heat, stirring occasionally and mashing with a spoon until reduced to a thick sauce. This will take about 20 minutes for zucchini, 35 for pumpkin. Season well, adding rather more nutmeg if you are using pumpkin.

Next fry the eggs. Heat olive oil, about ½ inch deep, in a saucepan until hot. Break one egg at a time into a cup, slipping the egg into the center of the oil, then tip the saucepan to make a deep-frying pool at the edge. At the same time roll the white around the egg with a skimmer or slotted spoon. It only takes 10 seconds to produce a puffy egg, so lift it out almost immediately. Arrange the eggs on the *pisto* and season lightly. Garnish the dish with a little parsley and serve.

WINDMILLS IN LA MANCHA *Don Quixote's stark, treeless tableland, bathed in shimmering, mysterious light, is punctuated only by the windmills which so readily evoke his exploits – and harness the power of the biting winds that sweep over the plateau.*

HUEVOS ESCALFADOS CON ALMEJAS

POACHED EGGS WITH CLAM SAUCE

This recipe, originally from the Poor Clares community of nuns, illustrates beautifully how humble food from one place can seem almost glamorous in another context. Mussels can also be used.

SERVES 4

2 lb littleneck clams, washed
1 cup fish stock, canned clam juice, or
clam-and-tomato juice
¾ cup dry white wine
1 onion, chopped
2 tablespoons butter
3 garlic cloves, finely chopped
3 tablespoons chopped parsley
1 tablespoon flour
salt and freshly ground black pepper
4 extra-large fresh eggs
vinegar for poaching
4 tostadas – slices of toasted or fried bread

Wash the clams in fresh water, discarding open ones. Heat the stock and wine with the chopped onion in a large pan with a lid. Put in enough clams to cover the bottom, cover and steam for a minute or so. When they open, scoop them out with a slotted spoon into a flameproof casserole, throw more clams into the pan and repeat. If they are small, pull off as many unoccupied top shells as you can. Reserve the liquid.

Put the butter into a saucepan and, when it is hot, stir in the garlic and parsley. Don't let the garlic color, but add the flour, stirring to cook it. Add the liquid from the clam pan, a little at a time, simmer gently, taste and season. Pour this sauce over the clams and let them simmer about 5 minutes.

Meanwhile, poach the eggs. Break the eggs individually into a cup and add one at a time to a wide pan of boiling water, with a few drops of vinegar (or use a poacher). Use a skimmer or slotted spoon to wrap the white around the yolk – the eggs will take about 4 minutes each to cook.

Put a *tostada* in each soup plate or dish, top with an egg and cover with clams and sauce. Large clams with both shells can be arranged around the egg, like the petals of a waterlily, but a sauce full of small ones is more traditional. When eating, use your tongue to scoop the clam off the shell and then spit out the latter.

PAELLA VALENCIANA

RICE WITH CHICKEN AND SEAFOOD

The most famous rice dish in the world, my recipe is adapted from the one José Ramos, chef at La Fonda in Marbella, makes in his own garden.

SERVES 6 – 8

2-lb chicken with giblets, or 3 small chicken legs plus a chicken carcass
1½ lb monkfish on the bone, or 1 lb white fish fillets, plus some fish bones
½ lb large shrimp in the shell
1 lb onions, chopped
tender pods from 10 oz shelled peas, or 1 celery stalk, chopped, plus 2 oz snow peas trimmed, in short lengths
1 bay leaf
⅔ cup white wine
20 saffron strands
1 lb littleneck clams or mussels, cleaned (see page 96)
½ lb baby squid, cleaned (see page 95)
16 oz canned tomatoes, with juice
about ⅔ cup olive oil
salt and freshly ground black pepper
½ lb sweet green peppers, seeded and cut in squares
5 fat garlic cloves, finely chopped
2½ cups Spanish medium-grain, or risotto, rice, washed
2 teaspoons paprika
¼ lb green beans, trimmed, in short lengths
½ cup cooked chickpeas (garbanzos) or Great Northern beans, or frozen lima beans
½ cup shelled peas
6 cooked shrimp in the shell, for garnish

Start by making a good stock. Strip off the meat of the chicken and cut into large chunks. Halve the legs, chopping through the bone with a heavy knife. Put the carcass (and giblets) into a stockpot.

Cut the fish into chunks about 2-inches wide and remove any skin. Peel the shrimp, putting the shells and fish debris in the stockpot. Add 1 chopped onion, half the pea pods, or celery stalk, and the bay leaf and

FRUIT AND VEGETABLE MARKET *Whatever is fresh and locally available can be gathered up and used in a* paella.

cover with water. Simmer 1 hour, then strain. Measure the liquid, add the wine and boil to reduce until you have about 5 cups liquid. Pour a little over the saffron in a cup and keep the rest ready in a saucepan.

Prepare the shellfish. Heat some of the stock in another saucepan and add half the clams or mussels. When they open, remove them and discard the shells. Cut the squid bodies into rings and keep the tentacles in a bunch. Check through the recipe and prepare all the ingredients, grouping things that are added together. Drain the tomato juice into the main stock and cut the tomatoes into strips. The recipe takes an hour from this point.

Use a *paella* pan about 16 inches across or a wide shallow casserole which will hold 4 quarts. Heat 4 tablespoons of oil over gentle heat and soften the remaining onions. Season the chicken pieces, increase the heat, and fry the chicken until golden. Add the sweet peppers and the remaining pods or snow peas and stir-fry about 5 minutes – more oil may be needed. Season well.

Add a little more oil, then toss the squid tentacles in it, so they stiffen. Reserve these for the garnish. Season the fish pieces and add them to the pan. (If you are not using a *paella* pan it is easier to do this in a separate skillet, with more oil.) Fry them on both sides and then add the squid rings.

Fry the garlic and add the rice to the main pan. Stir the rice in the oil and let it fry 3 – 4 minutes, sprinkling it with paprika. (If the fish was fried separately, fit it in now.) Add about a third of the hot stock to the pan, all the beans and peas with the peeled shrimp and shelled clams or mussels. Stir the rice for the last time, making sure that everything is evenly distributed around the pan, then tuck in the unshelled clams or mussels.

Arrange the tomato strips across the surface and pour in another third of the hot liquid. Reduce the heat to the minimum and start to shift the pan regularly, if the heat source is smaller than the pan bottom. (A thin pan, or a deep one, is best cooked in the oven preheated to 350° F from this point.)

Add the remaining stock and continue cooking 15 – 20 minutes. Test a rice grain: if it's cooked, garnish the top with the shelled shrimp and squid tentacles. Cover the top – traditionally it is wrapped in layers of newspaper – and let it sit 10 minutes for the rice to absorb the final liquid. In Spain, red wine is served with *paella* – try Faustino V *reserva*.

PAELLA DE VERDURAS DEL TIEMPO

PAELLA OF SPRING VEGETABLES

A *paella* can contain many things through the changing seasons – bacon, chard, tomatoes, white or black beans and turnips – usually with some part of the pig. Here is a pretty dish with the new season's vegetables. Fresh lima beans can be substituted for the asparagus, and chopped mushroom for the ham.

SERVES 6

¼ cup olive oil
1 small onion, chopped
6 oz raw ham, chopped small
2 garlic cloves, finely chopped
¼ cup chopped parsley
2 cups Spanish medium-grain, or risotto, rice, washed
3½ cups good stock
⅔ cup dry white wine
salt and freshly ground black pepper
¼ lb trimmed asparagus tips, in short lengths
¼ lb green beans, trimmed, in short lengths
2 small zucchini, thinly sliced
1 carrot, diced
1 tomato, without skin or seeds, diced
¼ lb snow peas, trimmed, snapped in half

Heat the oil in a *paella* pan or wide shallow flameproof casserole and fry the onion gently with the ham. When nearly soft, add the garlic. Add 2 tablespoons of parsley and the rice, stirring it in the oil for a minute or so.

Combine the stock and wine and taste it, adding seasoning as needed. If it is tasteless, boil to concentrate it, adding wine to make up the volume. Add a third to the rice, bring to the simmering point and add the asparagus. The rice takes 20–25 minutes from the moment the first batch of stock is added.

When the stock has been absorbed, add another third, with the beans, zucchini, carrot and tomato, and stir for the last time. Add the remaining stock with the snow peas. When the rice is done, cover the pan and let it stand, off the heat, for 5 minutes, then garnish with the remaining parsley. This is good served with slices of fried ham.

ARROZ A BANDA

FRAGRANT RICE FOLLOWED BY FISH AND ALIOLI

A banda means "apart" in the Valencian dialect, and in this recipe from the Alicante coast the rice is served first – without the fish that gives the stock in which it is cooked so much flavor. The fish then follows, hot, barely warm or cold, accompanied by a rich golden *alioli*. Different towns on the coast feature different fish for the second dish – at Catarroja, south of Valencia, it is gray mullet, for example. But it is generally agreed that rascasse and scorpion fish make the best base for the stock. I use a conger eel head or flounder skin and bones for stock, red mullet (goatfish) for color, a firm white fish like monkfish and a more delicately flavored one like hake or whiting. Ask the fish merchant to clean, descale and fillet the fish, but take home the heads and bones.

SERVES 6

5 lb whole fish, 3–4 kinds, calculating one third of the weight for fillets, and the rest for stock
2 onions, chopped
2 garlic cloves, finely chopped
1 cup canned tomatoes, with juice
1 sweet green pepper, seeded and chopped
2 bay leaves
10 black peppercorns, crushed
parsley stems plus ¼ cup finely chopped leaves
20 saffron strands
1½ cups dry white wine
12–18 new potatoes (½–¾ lb)
¼ lb tiny shrimp (optional)

FRAGRANT RICE
3 tablespoons olive oil
4 garlic cloves, finely chopped
2 cups Spanish medium-grain, or risotto, rice, washed
3 cups stock from the fish

EGG-YOLK ALIOLI
6 garlic cloves
½ teaspoon salt
2 egg yolks
scant 1 cup virgin olive oil

First make the stock. Rinse the fish heads and bones and put them in a stockpot with the onions, garlic, tomatoes, green pepper, bay leaves, crushed peppercorns and the stems from the parsley, snapped in several places. Cover with about 1½ quarts water. Cook 45 minutes from the time it starts simmering. Strain the stock; you will need about 1 quart for cooking the fish. Put the saffron in a cup and pour a little stock over it.

Make the *alioli*. Crush the garlic and salt to a paste in a mortar, or with the flat of a knife on a hard board, then move to a bowl. Add the egg yolks and whisk hard, adding the oil, a little at a time as for mayonnaise. This makes a thick butter (which can be thinned with 2 tablespoons of very strong, reduced fish stock).

Heat the stock with the saffron liquid and 1 cup wine and add the potatoes, and shrimp, if using. Cook 5 minutes, then add the fish fillets. Simmer gently, covered, 10 minutes.

Start the fragrant rice. Heat 2 tablespoons of oil in a *paella* pan or shallow flameproof casserole and add the garlic, then the rice. Stir-fry 3–4 minutes.

When the fish is ready, remove the fish fillets, potatoes and shellfish to a big shallow dish, and cover with foil. Strain the fish stock (there should be 1 quart) and reserve 1 cup in a saucepan for reheating the fish.

Pour half of the remaining stock onto the rice and stir. After 10 minutes add the rest of the stock and cook another 10–12 minutes. The liquid should all be absorbed. When the rice is done, turn off the heat, cover and let it stand 10 minutes. Serve the rice as it is or, at the most, garnished with a few soup shrimp.

To reheat the fish and potatoes, bring the reserved stock to a boil with the remaining white wine and pour over the fillets. Put in the oven preheated to 350° F for 10 minutes, then garnish with a little chopped parsley. Serve as the second course, accompanied by *alioli*.

Fine-flavored rice, without any distractions, can take a good *manzanilla* sherry. Partner it with a glass of cold water and something special from an *almacenista* – a maturer of wines who buys from small producers: Emilio Lustau ships such wines abroad.

After this, serve something a little refreshing with the fish, like a fruity white Rioja Navajas *blanco crianza*, made with 100% Viura, the Spanish white wine grape. Easier to find is CUNE's Monopole, which is fruity, with a modest amount of oakiness.

SELLING GARLIC AND ONIONS *An improvised hat provides extra protection from the sun.*

ARROZ CON COSTRA AL ESTILO DE ELCHE

RICE WITH A CRISP EGG CRUST

Unusually, this *paella* is baked in the oven and has a rich golden crust over the top, which is broken to release the fragrance of the rice and all the meats hidden in it – the "hidden treasures," as they have been called.

It's a good dish for the end of Christmas, as it can incorporate stuffing balls, a variety of different leftover meats and turkey stock. The recipe is given here, however, with freshly cooked meats, so you can judge the quantities.

SERVES 4 – 5

1 cup dried chickpeas (garbanzos), soaked in boiling water 1 hour (see page 11)
1½ – 2½ quarts stock
1 small dried chili pepper, seeded and chopped
¼ cup olive oil
1 onion, chopped
2 garlic cloves, finely chopped
½ lb ripe tomatoes, without skin or seeds, or 1 cup canned tomatoes with juice
salt and freshly ground black pepper
2½ cups Spanish medium-grain, or risotto, rice, washed
1½ teaspoons saffron powder
6 extra-large eggs

"HIDDEN TREASURES"
½ chicken or 3 chicken legs
¼ lb smoked ham in one piece
¼ lb cooking chorizo, morcilla or blood sausage, or other fresh spicy sausage
½ lb ground lean veal or pork
2 large pinches of ground cumin
¼ teaspoon ground cinnamon
beaten egg and flour, for coating
¼ lb lean boneless pork, cubed

Drain the chickpeas and cover generously with stock or water. Bring to a boil and simmer 30 minutes. When they start to soften, begin to make the "hidden treasures." Add the chicken, ham and sausages to the chickpeas with the dried chili pepper and simmer a further 30 minutes, when the chickpeas should be cooked. Remove the meats, leave to cool a little and cut into bite-sized chunks, discarding bones and skin.

Meanwhile, flavor the ground veal well with salt, cumin and cinnamon, and roll into large marble-sized balls. Coat the meatballs lightly in beaten egg, then move the balls to a plate covered with plenty of flour and shake it to and fro until the balls are coated.

In a wide shallow flameproof casserole that will hold 4 quarts, heat the oil and fry the veal balls over a high heat, shaking frequently so they color and crisp on all sides. Remove from the pan. Season the pork cubes and fry until well colored; reserve with the meatballs.

Next, make the flavoring for the rice. Soften the chopped onion in the pan, then add the garlic. Next, add the chopped tomatoes, season and let them reduce to a sauce. The recipe can be cooked in advance up to this point.

Heat the oven to 325° F. Add the rice to the hot tomato sauce and stir a minute or two. Drain the chickpeas and make up the cooking liquid with stock to 1½ quarts. Bring this to a boil, adding the saffron powder and taste it. This is the moment to add white wine (reducing the liquid again), paprika, even a bouillon cube, if the liquid is characterless, for this is the flavor the rice will assume presently.

Pour the stock into the rice and tomato mixture and bring slowly to a boil, stirring occasionally. Cook the rice 10 minutes. Add the chickpeas and all the prepared meats, distributing them around the pan. Bring back to a boil. Move the pan to the oven and cook a further 15 minutes.

Beat the eggs with a little salt and a tablespoon of water. Pour this over the rice, covering the whole surface. Turn up the oven to its highest heat and return the pan to bake 10 minutes. The dish should then rest, with the oven turned off and the door open, for about 10 minutes before serving. As there is such a medley of flavors in the dish, drink something simple like a less expensive red Rioja.

APARTMENT BLOCK *The infinitely varied greens of these wicker blinds add to the sense of rich and busy lives going on behind them.*

ARROZ CON JEREZ

RICE WITH SHERRY

A rich, medium-dry sherry gives this rice an intriguing southern accent – ideal to accompany a roast pork loin or tenderloin, cooked with a little garlic and a generous glass of the same sherry.

Another good side dish is made with all stock and the addition of 2 tablespoons each of toasted pine nuts and chopped almonds at the end.

SERVES 4

2 tablespoons olive oil
1 onion, chopped
2 garlic cloves, finely chopped
2 cups Spanish medium-grain, or risotto, rice, washed
1 cup amontillado sherry
1 quart good chicken stock, hot
salt and freshly ground black pepper
pinch of cayenne

Heat the oil in a *paella* pan or shallow flameproof casserole and fry the onion until soft and golden, adding the garlic near the end. Add the rice and turn in the oil for a minute or so. Add most of the sherry and let it bubble.

Sample the stock, adding salt, pepper and cayenne as needed, so that the seasoning is very lively. Add to the rice, bring to the simmering point, then turn down the heat. Cook 20 minutes without stirring. Turn off the heat, sprinkle with the remaining sherry and cover with a lid. Let the rice steam gently 10 minutes, to absorb the last drops of liquid.

FIDEUÀ DE MARISCOS

PASTA WITH SEAFOOD

Somehow pasta has taken over from rice in this seafood dish from the Costa Brava, which is made in a *paella* pan. Combine these shellfish with rice, and the dish becomes a *paella de mariscos*. The recipe is made from whatever shellfish are available in the market.

This is by far the easiest – and cheapest – of the big, bravura shellfish dishes. The quantity can be multiplied three or four times for a party, as it can be cooked successfully in a deeper pan – unlike *paella*.

The traditional pasta of Catalonia is *fideos* – only about 1 inch long and the thickness of fine spaghetti. However, I look for a pasta needing 8 – 10 minutes' cooking, for this is the ideal time to let the shellfish flavors blend into the stock and then into the pasta itself.

SERVES 4

2 tablespoons olive oil
1 onion, finely chopped
2 garlic cloves, finely chopped
¼ lb ripe tomato, without skin or seeds
pinch of cayenne or ½ small dried chili pepper, seeded
1 bay leaf
3 cups good fish stock (see page 16)
1 cup dry white wine
14 oz fine spaghetti, broken in short lengths
10 oz hake or whiting fillet, cubed
4 langoustines or jumbo shrimp
6 oz small squid, cleaned and sliced (see page 95)
½ lb medium shrimp
½ lb littleneck clams or small mussels, cleaned (see page 96)
lemon wedges to garnish (optional)

Heat the oil in a shallow flameproof casserole and fry the onion gently until soft, adding the garlic toward the end. Put in the tomato with the cayenne or chili pepper and bay leaf, stirring occasionally until soft and reduced.

Add the stock and wine and bring to a boil. Add the pasta, hake cubes and jumbo shrimp and cook 5 minutes. Add the squid and other shellfish and cook another 5 minutes or until the pasta is done and all the liquid is absorbed. *Alioli* (see page 54) is sometimes stirred in at the end or accompanies it.

The rich buttery-tasting Chardonnay grapes are part of a new style of winemaking in Catalonia, and make whites that will stand up to all the different flavors of this dish. Look for Raimat Chardonnay from Lérida or the slightly pineapple-y Torres Gran Viña Sol, with about half Chardonnay grapes.

CANELONES CON LANGOSTINOS

FRIED CANNELLONI WITH SHRIMP

Cannelloni are a popular part of Spanish cuisine and are eaten all over the country with a variety of fillings. These unusual cannelloni from the Costa Brava are crisp on the outside and the meltingly creamy middle has a real taste of the sea. They consist almost entirely of delicious fat shrimp, just held together by a little sauce and the cannelloni are then deep-fried.

A hot appetizer that can be made almost entirely in advance, the dish also makes a good late-night supper for two or three.

SERVES 4

1½ lb large shrimp in the shell, or ½ lb peeled shrimp
¼ cup dry vermouth (or ¼ chicken bouillon cube, plus a little paprika and nutmeg)
1 bay leaf (optional)
⅔ – 1 cup milk

2 tablespoons butter
2 tablespoons flour
1 extra-large egg
salt and freshly ground black pepper
8 cannelloni tubes, plus a few spares
olive oil for deep frying

BEER BATTER
1 extra-large egg
2 tablespoons butter
¾ cup flour
½ – ⅔ cup light beer
a little freshly grated nutmeg

If you have shrimp in the shell, peel them, putting the heads and shells into a pan with the vermouth and bay leaf. Add water almost to cover and simmer very gently 30 minutes. Strain the stock, return to the pan and boil to reduce to about ¼ cup. Add milk to bring up to nearly 1 cup and warm it. If using peeled shrimp, warm the larger quantity of milk with the bouillon cube and flavor carefully with a little paprika and nutmeg.

Melt the butter in a small pan and stir in the flour. Cook 1 minute, then stir in the milk. Bring to a boil slowly, stirring, and cook 1 minute or so. Take off the heat, beat in the egg, seasoning to taste, and leave until cold.

Bring some water to a boil in a small roasting pan and put in 8 cannelloni tubes (plus 2 – 3 spares if using Italian quick-cook cannelloni, as these tend to split). Cook 8 minutes, shaking the pan occasionally to make sure they are not sticking, then drain carefully.

Chop the peeled shrimp coarsely, mix with the white sauce – just enough to make the shrimp adhere – and stuff 8 cannelloni tubes. Chill well.

About 15 mintues before serving, make the batter. Beat the egg and melted butter into the flour. Gradually beat in the beer to make a smooth batter and season with nutmeg, pepper and salt. Heat the oil, at least 1½ to 2 inches deep, in a wide pan. Dip the stuffed cannelloni, one at a time on a slotted spatula, into the batter. Slide into the oil, allowing 10 seconds between each one, as they are cold and the oil must reheat. When 4 are frying in a row, turn them over gently with a slotted spoon. When golden on both sides, lift them out in the original order and drain on paper towels. Fry the second batch and serve promptly. A delicate young white wine, like the local Marqués de Alella, which is slightly spritzy, makes a good partner.

VEGETABLES
AND SALADS

*All the sun-drenched colors and richness of
Spain seem to have been absorbed by the
country's vegetables and the simple but
exuberant dishes they produce.*

ENSALADA DE NARANJAS VALENCIANAS *left (p 74)*,
TOMATES RELLENOS A LA ALICANTINA *right (p 71)*.

THE WONDERFUL IMMEDIACY OF SPANISH food is seen at its best in Spanish vegetables, which reach the plate in the shortest possible time. Think of the popular salad *ensalada mixta*, with great chunks of sunny tomato, lettuce just hours from the field, pungent, juicy onion rings and a scattering of olives. The dressing is left to you: simple and satisfying!

The colors of the vegetables, their freshness and generous size, make market shopping in Spain an extraordinary pleasure. Huge bunches of chard, for example, with glossy dark leaves and pearl-white stalks, the size of a small wheat sheaf, bright red heaps of sweet peppers, crates of lettuce, bales of bay leaves – everything comes in generous quantities but at small cost. No wonder Spain has become the market garden of Europe.

Every vegetable is valued. It's not a sideshow to the main dish, but a separate course, on its own plate. The vocabulary reflects this attention: where English only has "bean," for example, there are 14 or more Spanish words, distinguishing the different types. There are two nouns for sweet potatoes, according to the color inside. Cabbage is *col*, *berza*, *repollo* or *lombarda* according to its shape and color. There are also a host of regional words, which reflect the local feeling that just there, in that corner of Spain, grow the best peas, or artichokes, or beans in the world.

Vegetables are seasonal, which adds to their pleasure. The range is local but may include rarities unobtainable elsewhere, like the cardoon, cousin of the artichoke, whose stalks are eaten on Christmas Eve. There are also wild foods like spring asparagus and palmetto hearts, cut from small palms at Easter. *Tagarnina* is a thistle popular in *tortillas* in winter in the south. Fat capers, *alcaparras*, grow on the mountains behind the south and east coasts, and make ideal partners for fried fish like *mero*, grouper, and shark.

At the base of the vegetable pot there are often chickpeas. *Garbanzos* were introduced to Spain by the Carthaginians, and the Roman writer, Plautus, ridiculed the chickpea-eating Spaniards, just as Shakespeare mocked the Welsh for eating toasted cheese. This curious dried pea, shaped "like a widow's nose and a dress-maker's backside," is attractively chewy, and fairs also sell them as a snack, already cooked and salted.

But the "meat of Spain" is the olive. Looking out from the beautiful Giralda tower of what was once the Seville mosque, there is a sea of olive trees, as far as the eye can see, in the flat Guadalquivir valley. The Arabs did not introduce the tree, but they planted them more widely and spread the taste for olive oil, one of the basic flavors of Spanish cooking.

The Moors ruled over at least a part of Spain for almost 1,000 years. "A land which hovers between Europe and Africa, between the hat and the turban," Richard Ford called it in *Gatherings from Spain*, in 1846. The Moors introduced rice and irrigated the south, planting citrus fruits and almonds, and starting the system that now supports the green beans and the mint, the melons, tomatoes and the garlic.

They also brought new vegetables, like eggplants, from the East, and in the kitchen their legacy is very visible, in the many words that have the prefix *al*. *Almuerzo*, *albóndigas*, *almíbar*, *almirez* – lunch, meat-balls, sugar syrup and the brass mortar – are but a few. The mortar and pestle has became a basic adjunct to soup-and-sauce-making, crushing fried bread, toasted almonds and garlic cloves. "That gay prelude to an Andalusian meal," Gerald Brenan called the noise of pounding. With their thoughtfulness about spicing and textures, the introduction of cumin and cinnamon, the fondness for saffron, and an understanding of sweet and savory, the Moors made Spain the European center of civilized cooking.

The second great wave of change in Spain was the introduction of vegetables from America. John Gerrard's *Herbal*, in 1597, remarks in wonder on Spanish tomatoes. With them came sweet peppers and chilies, at first regarded only as a flavoring for tomatoes. Spanish cooks now choose judiciously between the different types of capsicum needed for a dish, just as Americans might specify a particular apple or lettuce.

The potato, too, found its first European home near Seville, where the account books of the local nuns for 1576 record their purchase. The many varieties of kidney beans were each adopted in different parts of Spain, augmenting the tough local broad or fava bean. These new vegetables transformed the Spanish diet, and vegetables throughout Europe were never to be the same again.

COLIFLOR AL ESTILO DE BADAJOZ

FRIED CAULIFLOWER

Simple and surprisingly tasty – as food from poor regions like Extremadura often is – this is also a good way to use up leftover cauliflower.

SERVES 4

1 large head cauliflower
1 garlic clove
½ teaspoon salt
6 tablespoons wine vinegar
freshly ground black pepper
2 tablespoons finely chopped parsley
flour for coating
2 extra-large eggs, beaten
olive oil for frying

Separate the cauliflower into florets, trimming back the smaller stems and splitting any larger bunches. Cook them 5 minutes in a generous quantity of boiling salted water, then drain well.

Mash the garlic to a paste with the salt, using the flat side of a knife or a mortar and pestle. Mix the vinegar into the paste and pour over the cauliflower in a wide bowl. Sprinkle with pepper and parsley and let marinate 30 minutes, turning the cauliflower once.

Turn the florets in flour on a plate, then dip in beaten egg. Fry in hot oil, turning them over until golden on all sides. If there is parsley left in the marinade bowl, this can be sprinkled on top. The cauliflower may also be served with a tomato sauce.

PIMIENTOS CON NATA

GRILLED SWEET RED PEPPERS WITH CREAM

Aragon is known for its peppers: long, pointed, spicy *pimientos de piquillo*, and this is the ingredient I most regret not being able to buy outside Spain. This simple dish is surprisingly effective, even when made with sweet bell peppers. It comes from the hilltop town of Sos del Rey Católico, famous as the birthplace of Ferdinand of Aragon, who united Spain by marrying Isabella of Castile in 1474.

SERVES 6

6 sweet red peppers
¾ cup whipping cream
pinch of sugar
pinch of salt

Grill the peppers over coals or under the broiler about 20 minutes, giving them a quarter turn every 5 minutes, until they are charred on all sides. Put them in a plastic bag for 10 minutes, then strip off the charred skins and pull out and discard the stems and seeds. Do this on a plate to catch all the sweet juices.

Trim off the top and bottom of each pepper and open them to remove the last seeds. Purée the trimmings and juices in a blender.

Arrange the peppers on a serving plate, or preferably individual dishes, and reheat in a low oven or under the broiler. Heat the cream, stir in the purée, plus the sugar and salt, then pour it over the peppers and serve immediately.

CALÇOTS AMB ROMESCO

GRILLED SCALLIONS
WITH ROMESCO SAUCE

I was about to leave out the recipe for these most delicious of barbecue vegetables when I realized that every Chinese store sells the fat scallions, or green onions, that the recipe needs. In Valls, in the province of Tarragona, the coming of spring and warmer weather is marked by *la calçotada*, a party out in the fields to pick this special, juicy onion.

Toasted on a barbecue, until black on the outside, and eaten with swordfish, lightly dressed with sherry vinegar, or arranged between trout under the broiler, they make a wonderful fish accompaniment. In season, however, they are a dish by themselves with a traditional sauce. Bibs are often provided as removing the outside can be a messy business.

The onions are produced by plucking out every central sprouting shoot from stored onions, at the end of the year. The shoots are then planted, watered once and picked a couple of months later.

SERVES 4

12–16 big scallions, about 1 inch in diameter, or the
fattest you can buy
1 tablespoon melted butter
1 tablespoon olive oil
Romesco *Sauce (see page 88)*

Cut off the soft green tips and brush the onions with the mixed butter and oil. Grill over coals or under the broiler 15 minutes, turning once, until black on the outside. Everyone peels his or her own, so provide plenty of napkins. Serve with *romesco* sauce.

MOUNTAIN FARM *The rich variations of the Spanish climate and landscape, encompassing stark, arid plains and lush, green hills, are one factor behind Spain's extraordinarily diverse cuisine.*

ACELGAS CON PASAS Y PIÑONES

SPINACH WITH RAISINS
AND PINE NUTS

This is a popular dish around the Mediterranean, and nowadays it is commonly made, as here, with the leaves of chard or with spinach, which is easier to find. However, I have an old Malagueñan recipe, which uses the white chard ribs only, cut into 2-inch lengths, with the local fat raisins.

SERVES 4

¼ cup raisins (seedless muscatels are best)
2 tablespoons olive oil
3 tablespoons pine nuts
1 onion, finely chopped
1 garlic clove, finely chopped
2 lb bulk spinach or chard, more if stalks are big
salt and freshly ground black pepper
4 tostadas – *slices of toast or fried bread*

Soak the raisins in boiling water to plump them. Heat the oil and fry the pine nuts, turning them constantly until golden. Remove and add the onion. Fry the onion until golden, then add the garlic.

Wash the spinach or chard, stripping out the stems. Cook spinach in only the water clinging to the leaves, in a covered pan, turning the top to the bottom occasionally – it takes about 10 minutes. Chard is tougher – cook in boiling water 15 mintues. Drain and chop.

Stir the chopped leaves into the onion, adding the drained raisins and nuts; season and heat through. Serve with *tostadas*.

ROVELLONS AL AJILLO

WILD MUSHROOMS WITH GARLIC

In September in Catalonia and the Basque country, serious-looking men swarm into the mountains to pick mushrooms. *Rovellon* is the Catalan name for Spain's best-loved mushroom, called *níscalo* in Castilian – a stunning golden yellow underneath. Big ones become cup-shaped, like communion chalices, pleated on the underside. A true *rovellon* will "bleed" from the stem when cut — single drops of bloodlike juice reminiscent of a medieval miracle – and this gives them their English name of "bleeding milk cap." In New England, these mushrooms are called *crimini*.

The Spaniards would certainly allow $\frac{1}{2}$ pound a head, but if you can find wild mushrooms like chanterelles, 6 ounces is enough for two. Don't over-cook or over-chop wild things, but treat them gently and let them show off their natural fragrance of the woods. Brown mushrooms are the best cultivated substitute.

An old-fashioned appetizer for four served with, or on, fried bread, it can be accompanied with chilled *palo cortado*, a medium-dry sherry, in sweetness between an *amontillado* and an *oloroso*. The dish also makes a delicious supper for two.

SERVES 2

1 tablespoon butter
1 tablespoon olive oil
1 small garlic clove, finely chopped
about $\frac{1}{4}$ lb wild or cultivated brown mushrooms
salt and freshly ground black pepper
1 tablespoon finely chopped parsley

Heat the butter and oil in a skillet and add the chopped garlic and sliced mushrooms. Fry them quickly – they are very meaty and don't lose their shape or make juice in the pan. Turn the mushrooms over occasionally with a wooden spoon. Season and sprinkle them with parsley.

HABAS RONDEÑAS

LIMA BEANS WITH HAM, RONDA-STYLE

Ronda, in Andalusia, is famous throughout Spain as the place where Francisco Romero laid down the rules of bullfighting in the 18th century, and nothing is too good for fighting bulls, who are fed for the contest on broad or fava beans. These beans also combine particularly well with *serrano*, the local raw ham. Tender frozen baby lima beans, which are available in every supermarket, are an excellent substitute.

SERVES 6

6 oz raw ham, smoked ham or Canadian bacon
$\frac{1}{4}$ cup olive oil
1 cup chopped mild Spanish onion
1 garlic clove, finely chopped
2 lb frozen baby lima beans
4 extra-large eggs
salt and freshly ground black pepper
1 cup chopped parsley

Dice the ham (or cut the bacon into strips). Heat the oil in a flameproof casserole and add the onion and ham or bacon. Fry very gently until the bacon has given off its fat and the onion is soft. Add the garlic toward the end.

Stir in the frozen beans, cover, turn down the heat and cook until tender, stirring occasionally – this should take about 12 minutes.

Meanwhile, hard-cook the eggs 10 minutes and chop them. Season the beans generously, stir in the chopped eggs and heat through. Stir in the parsley. In summer, when parsley is almost unobtainable in the south of Spain, diced sweet red pepper or tomato may be used instead to garnish the dish.

VINES IN LA MANCHA *Low-growing vines cover much of La Mancha, Spain's largest single wine-producing area.*

LA RIOJA ALTA (overleaf) *The higher part of the Rioja area, the Rioja Alta, has a cooler, wetter climate and a soil which yields the acidity necessary to produce its distinctive wines.*

MENESTRA A LA BILBAINA

BILBAO MIXED VEGETABLE POT

A dish celebrating the new vegetables of spring, *menestra* is made all along the northern coast of Spain, as far as the French Basque country.

A seemingly simple dish, it can achieve considerable sophistication in the hands of a good cook. In Asturias, fried potatoes and ham are added at the end, while in Navarre the artichoke bases, and lengths of chard stalk, are floured and fried for contrasting texture.

SERVES 6

2 tablespoons diced ham fat or olive oil
1 onion, chopped
3 garlic cloves, finely chopped
6 tablespoons chopped parsley
¾ cup dry white wine
¼ lb cooked ham, diced
1¼ cups light meat or chicken stock
1½ cups shelled fresh broad (fava) beans
1½ cups shelled fresh peas, reserving a few tender pods
the trimmed bases of 4 artichokes (see page 103)
½ lb green beans, trimmed, in short lengths
½ cup young carrots, in short lengths
salt and freshly ground black pepper
2 hard-cooked eggs, chopped

Heat the ham fat or oil in a flameproof casserole and soften the onion, adding the garlic and 2 tablespoons of parsley toward the end. Remove the onion to a blender and reduce to a purée with a little of the wine. Add the diced ham to the casserole and fry gently.

Bring a saucepan of salted water to a boil; add the stock to the casserole and bring to a boil. Then cook the vegetables in the following sequence: add the broad (fava) beans to the casserole, at the same time putting the peas (plus a few tender pods) into the simmering water. After 10 minutes add the quartered artichoke bases to the casserole and the remaining vegetables to the simmering water, and cook 10 minutes.

Drain the vegetables that were cooked in water and add them to the casserole. Add the remaining wine and the onion purée, warming the liquid and turning the vegetables gently. Check the seasoning and serve in soup plates with a little of the juices, sprinkled with chopped egg and the remaining parsley.

JUDÍAS BLANCAS A LO TÍO LUCAS

UNCLE LUKE'S MILDLY SPICED BEANS

Behind this warming dish of spicy beans stands the comfortable figure of a barkeeper called Uncle Luke. He invented it in the early years of the 19th century for the poor sailors who frequented Cadiz, living on credit while they waited to be paid off at the end of each voyage. Uncle Luke then moved to Madrid, where he opened a hostelry, and here his excellent beans achieved national fame.

SERVES 6

2¼ cups dried Great Northern or other white beans
5 oz thick, fat bacon or a smoked pork chop
2 tablespoons of olive oil
2 large onions, chopped
1 garlic bulb, cloves peeled and finely chopped
2 tablespoons tomato paste
1 bay leaf
2 teaspoons paprika
1 tablespoon vinegar
¼ teaspoon ground cumin
pinch of ground cloves
1 tablespoon finely chopped parsley
¼ teaspoon ground white pepper
1 teaspoon salt

Soak the beans 1 hour in boiling water, or overnight in plenty of cold water.

Cut the fat off the bacon or smoked pork chop and fry the onions and chopped fat in the olive oil in the bottom of a bean pot or flameproof casserole. After 10 minutes add the lean meat, chopped to the size of small soup croutons, then the garlic. Drain the beans and add them to the pot with the remaining ingredients and enough water to cover them well.

Simmer 1¼–1½ hours, until the beans are soft, checking occasionally that they are not sticking or drying out. There should be enough liquid to give each person a couple of spoonfuls with the beans. Check the seasonings and serve as an appetizer in soup plates. The beans also make a good side dish with fatty meat like bacon and sausages, or roast shoulder of lamb.

MIGAS DE PASTOR

CRISP FRIED BREAD CRUMBS

Bread plays a large part in the Spanish diet, and very good bread it is, crisp and fresh. Better, the Spaniards would say, than French bread, which is the perfect substitute. Not so long ago in country places 2 pounds or so a day was a common portion, as an accompaniment to vegetables or meat, and a mopper-up of sauces.

Bread is never eaten stale. Such value is placed on it that dressers in old country kitchens have a special drawer for yesterday's bread, which is then used for cooking. Crumbs thicken sauces, slices lie at the bottom of soup plates and *tostadas* may accompany vegetables – try them fried in the red fat from *manteca colorada* (see page 28). Though Spanish bread is white, a brown loaf is the better choice, if the only alternative is the sliced white soft-textured variety.

These savory crumbs are eaten all over Spain, though particularly associated with Aragon. In poor places like Extremadura they are used to eke out cooked vegetables – or accompany eggs and bacon. Gerald Brenan's landlord ate them with sardines and chocolate sauce – together! This recipe came originally from the Military Academy at Zaragoza.

SERVES 4

4 thick slices of bread, cut from a loaf, stale
enough to be firm
salt and freshly ground black pepper
oil for frying
2 garlic cloves, bruised with the flat of a knife
pisto (see page 50) or samfaina (see page 89)
(optional)

Cut off the crusts and cut the bread into ½-inch cubes. Sprinkle with water, season with salt and pepper and wrap up overnight in a napkin.

Half an hour before serving, heat the oil with the garlic cloves. When it smokes, discard the garlic and add the crumbs. Cook them 12–15 minutes, moving them constantly. Serve them very hot, as a partner to a tomato stew – they are also frequently served with bacon and eggs.

TOMATES RELLENOS A LA ALICANTINA

STUFFED TOMATOES FROM ALICANTE

A simple stuffed tomato dish, with spinach, orange juice and nuts, from the east coast.

SERVES 4

1 lb bulk spinach
4 – 5 tablespoons butter
4 large ripe tomatoes, over ½ lb each
6 – 8 oz raw ham, smoked ham or Canadian bacon
1 tablespoon olive oil (if using ham)
grated zest and juice of 1 orange
salt and freshly ground black pepper
½ cup blanched almonds

Wash and drain the spinach, stripping out the stems. Wash again, tearing up bigger leaves. Put 2 tablespoons of butter into a large pan and cook the spinach in the water clinging to the leaves, with the lid on. After 5 minutes, remove the lid, turn the top leaves to the bottom and cook 10 minutes more, uncovered.

Meanwhile, heat the oven to 350° F. Halve the tomatoes across and scoop out the insides with a spoon. Arrange the halves in a large greased dish. If you are using raw ham, put 1 tablespoon each of butter and olive oil into a saucepan, heat and add the chopped ham. If you are using smoked ham or bacon, cut off and dice the fat; add 2 tablespoons of fat cubes to the pan. Heat until the fat runs, then add the cubed lean meat. Drain the spinach and chop it well – a board with a groove around it is useful to catch the juices. Add to the pan, turning it in the fat. Add the grated orange zest and the juice and season well.

Melt 2 tablespoons of butter in a small pan and toss the almonds until they are colored. Remove and chop them, then stir back into the butter. Spoon the spinach mixture into the tomato halves and top with chopped almonds. Bake 20 minutes. A red Valdepeñas *reserva*, made from Cenibel, which is the best of the Rioja grapes, will stand up well to the spinach.

PATATAS PICANTES

SPICY FRIED POTATOES

Potatoes fried in paprika are popular all over Spain and are one of the best-known dishes outside the country. This way of making them incorporates a little trick from the Canary Islands, where the potatoes are cooked in seawater – theoretically until it evaporates – which leaves them crusted with salt and tasting delicious. The potatoes are then finished simply: just fried in oil and paprika. They are excellent with pork chops.

SERVES 4

1 – 1½ lb new potatoes, each about 2 oz, scrubbed but not peeled
2 tablespoons coarse salt
¼ cup olive oil
4 fat garlic cloves
½ small dried chili pepper, seeded and chopped, or a pinch of mild chili powder
1 – 2 teaspoons paprika

Choose a wide saucepan and put in as many potatoes as will fit tightly in a single layer. Cover with cold water, add the salt and bring to a boil. Cover and cook 20 – 25 minutes until done but not breaking up. Drain and peel or not as you wish, then cut into slices.

Heat the oil in a skillet. Bruise the whole garlic cloves by pressing on them with the flat of a knife and add to the pan with the chopped, dried chili pepper, if using. When the garlic browns, discard the garlic and chili pepper.

Add the potato slices over medium-high heat. When they start to color around the edges, sprinkle with the paprika, and chili powder if using, and turn in the pan for a couple of minutes more. Because there is no chopped garlic in this dish, which would burn, the potatoes can wait in the pan over very low heat for 10 – 15 minutes.

GARBANZOS Y CHORIZOS

CHICKPEA AND SAUSAGE STEW

A dish from the chilly, wet region of Galicia, guaranteed to keep out the cold: my household eats it when we have been too long without Spanish food. Tolosa, in the Basque country, is famous for a similar dish made with black beans, while in Burgos pinto beans are used. Use whatever spicy sausages you can find – *morcilla* is often included as half the amount. With the modern short cuts of tomato juice and canned pimientos, the spicy base is very quick to make.

A good idea for supper with green salad and red wine, this is one of the few dried legume dishes that reheats successfully. A little can be used in a *tortilla* and it's also good cold.

SERVES 4–6

2½ cups dried chickpeas (garbanzos), soaked 1 hour in boiling water, or overnight in cold water
about 3½ cups unsalted stock, or one-third tomato juice, two-thirds water
1 large onion, chopped
2 tablespoons olive oil
1 lb cooking chorizos or other fresh spicy sausages, mild and hot together, in chunks
2 garlic cloves, finely chopped
4 oz canned pimientos or 2 tablespoons tomato paste (but not if using juice), plus 1 teaspoon paprika
salt and freshly ground black pepper

Drain the chickpeas, then simmer them in 1½ times their own volume of stock for ¾ to 1½ hours (depending on the brand, see page 11) until tender.

Fry the onion in the oil very slowly until soft, adding the sausage chunks after 10 minutes. Fry them 20 minutes, turning them over occasionally. As they give off fat, add the garlic. When they are cooked, add them and their juices to the chickpeas.

Drain the pimientos, cut into strips and stir in (or add the tomato paste and paprika). Simmer 10 minutes, season and serve.

GARBANZOS Y CHORIZOS *left,* MENESTRA A LA BILBAINA *right (p 67).*

ALCACHOFAS CON DOS SALSAS

ARTICHOKES WITH TWO SAUCES

The Spaniards admire the beautiful shape of artichokes and don't cut the leaves unnecessarily. It's more convenient for the eater, however, if the hairy chokes are removed before they come to table. The cup this makes is then filled with mayonnaise, and there is vinaigrette for dipping the outside leaves. The same two sauces are often served with the white asparagus from Rioja, which is canned and sent all over the country.

SERVES 4

4 large globe artichokes
1 garlic clove, finely chopped
1 tablespoon finely chopped parsley
⅔ cup mayonnaise (see page 78)
½ cup olive oil
3 tablespoons wine vinegar
salt and freshly ground black pepper

Snap off the stems; with large tough artichokes this will bring away most of the stringy fibers underneath. Trim the base almost flat, removing little leaves. This will tell you how tender the artichokes are, and give you a better idea of cooking time. Cook tender heads 20 minutes, and large tough ones 40 minutes in plenty of salted boiling water. They will stay green if cooked without a lid. Drain them upside down for 10 minutes to cool a little.

To prepare them for the table, start by pulling out the center leaves. When a soft, lighter cone becomes visible under the first leaves to go, hold the artichoke firm and pull the whole cone out. Underneath is the inedible hairy choke – scoop it out with a spoon. For decoration turn the cone of small leaves over and lodge it in the artichoke to keep the cup open.

Eat barely warm or cold. To serve, stir a little garlic and parsley into the mayonnaise and fill each cup. Make a vinaigrette with the oil, vinegar and seasoning and pour a little on each individual plate. Eat the outside leaves, dipping each base into vinaigrette. Eat the inside ones – and finally the base itself – with mayonnaise. Remember to put out a plate to use for the discarded leaves.

ENSALADA DE NARANJAS VALENCIANAS

VALENCIAN ORANGE AND ONION SALAD

A Spanish pantry salad, from winter ingredients, this seems to have gone out of fashion somewhat, now that lettuce and tomatoes are on sale year-round. It is nevertheless excellent for adding a splash of color to any meal and wonderful before a lamb stew. If salad greens are available, decorate the salad with lettuce or curly endive around the outside.

SERVES 6

1 red onion, or ½ mild Spanish onion
4 large oranges
lettuce (optional)

2 tablespoons red wine vinegar
6 tablespoons olive oil
salt and freshly ground black pepper
pinch of sugar
a few ripe olives

Slice the onion as thin as possible and push it out into rings. Peel the oranges, removing the membrane from the outside of the segments with the pith. Slice into rings and remove the seeds. Arrange the orange and onion slices in a salad bowl. If using a deep bowl, line it with lettuce first, so a frill appears around the edge. If the bowl is wide and shallow, roll the lettuce leaves in wads, slice across them and arrange the ribbons around the edge.

Use the next 5 ingredients to make a vinaigrette and pour over the salad. Scatter with ripe olives and let the salad stand 30 minutes, for the flavors to mingle, before serving.

ESCALIVADA CON ANCHOAS

BAKED EGGPLANT AND SWEET RED PEPPER SALAD WITH ANCHOVIES

I suspect the reason why this exotic dish is unknown outside Spain is because its subtle colors photograph so badly. The eggplant turns a smoky gray-green and becomes unrecognizably soft, with prominent seeds which look figlike. Spanish virgin oils, like Nunez de Prado or Sierra de Segura, are very fruity, and so make a good dressing.

Escalivar is the Catalan verb for "cooking over the embers" and, on a barbecue, the vegetables pick up a smoky flavor. They make a popular garnish for grilled steak. Tomatoes and potatoes can be included too, and everything puréed (with a little cayenne if not using Spanish peppers). The resulting cream is chilled and served as an appetizer or as a sauce for fried sole.

SERVES 4

4 sweet red peppers
4 small eggplants, about 7 oz each
2 oz canned anchovies, drained
¼ cup virgin Spanish olive oil

Heat the oven to 400° F. Bake the peppers and eggplants on the wire rack 1 hour, turning them over at half time. When they are soft, transfer the peppers to a plastic bag.

Remove the stems from the eggplants; the dark skin will come away easily. They will be soft and silky in texture, and only a quarter of their original weight. Split them into 4 to show off their exotic seeds. Remove the skin from the peppers, discarding stems and seeds, and halve them lengthwise.

Arrange an eggplant and a pepper quarter on each plate (either side by side, or with the pepper on top like a sandwich) and crisscross with anchovies. Dribble a little virgin olive oil over the salad.

DRYING BEANS *The number and variety of different beans in Spain – which are eaten fresh as well as dried – are truly astonishing. Each locality has its own, prized specialty.*

AMANIDA CATALANA

CATALAN ARRANGED SALAD

Amanida is the Catalan word for "salad" and comes from *amanir*, "to season," just as our own word comes from *sal*, "to salt." It is different every time, according to what is available.

We eat this salad for lunch most days in hot weather, choosing one group of ingredients only, with 3 or 4 items. The choice of ingredients is wide: for example, white canned asparagus can be substituted for the artichoke hearts, and goes well with mayonnaise and anchovies. Another happy combination is red mullet, cooked and dressed *en escabeche* (see page 118), with buttery avocados.

Arranged like the spokes of a wheel on a large plate, *amanida catalana* makes a dramatic buffet dish, or centerpiece for the first course of a dinner party.

SERVES 6

6 bunches of tentacles cut from 1 lb small squid, cleaned (see page 95) and rinsed
2 tablespoons olive oil
16 oz canned artichoke hearts, drained
2 cups ripe tomatoes, without skin or seeds, chopped into big dice
½ cup vinaigrette
6 thin slices jamón serrano or prosciutto
½ tablespoon very finely chopped parsley
18 small ripe olives, cured in oil, about 2 oz
2 cans 4½-oz sardines in oil, well drained
3 canned pimientos, well drained
3 hard-cooked eggs, sliced
1 tablespoon large capers
½ cup thick mayonnaise (see page 78)
12 king-sized green olives, about 3 oz
about ¼ lb boiled shrimp in the shell
leaves from a head of curly endive or lollo bianco lettuce
flat parsley leaves

Blot the squid tentacles well on paper towels. Heat the oil in a small skillet and put in the tentacles, cut side down, so that they open like flowers. Fry them 1 minute on each side, flipping them over so the other side turns pink. Drain on paper towels and reserve.

Cut the artichoke hearts into thirds lengthwise and dress them, and the tomatoes, lightly with vinaigrette before you start the arrangement.

Arrange all the items on a large plate about 14 inches across – I used a big glass shell-plate – or on individual salad plates. The various salads look best kept in groups, rather than dotted around. Spokes of a wheel look good on a big round plate and a fan shape on individual plates.

Cut the raw ham in half across the middle and roll up each piece so it has a frill of fat at the top. Arrange the ham rolls in a wedge and heap the tomato next to them. Scatter lightly with chopped parsley and pile the ripe olives next to the tomato.

Arrange the sardines all together, overlapping slightly in a wedge, with the tails toward the center of the plates. Slice the pimiento in strips, and arrange next to them. The two red salads – pimiento and tomato – should always be separated.

Put the sliced eggs next to the sardines. Add the capers to the mayonnaise and pile half over the eggs, with the green king olives toward the center. Add the artichoke hearts as another wedge.

Arrange the shrimp on the outside of the last section, with the squid flowers inside them. Finally, tuck a tiny bunch of endive or lettuce between each section on the outside rim of the plate, and put some flat parsley leaves in the center. The whole thing is so ornamental and delicious, I would add to the festive mood with Cava, the sparkling Catalan wine made by the champagne method. Codorníu and Raimat both have Cavas made from Chardonnay grapes.

PIRIÑACA

SWEET PEPPER SALAD WITH TUNA AND EGG

The dressing of this chopped salad has a much longer history in Spain than the vegetables it garnishes. Far older than mayonnaise, it is made with oil and the yolks of hard-cooked eggs.

Jaén, in the north of Andalusia, is famous for a very similar salad called *pipirrana*, which contains cucumber as well, but not necessarily tuna. Well chilled – and so a hairsbreadth away from *gazpacho* – *pipirrana* accompanies slices of raw ham.

SERVES 6 – 8

3 medium or 2 extra-large eggs
7 oz canned water-packed tuna, well drained
3 small sweet green peppers, stem and seeds removed
3 fat ripe tomatoes, without skin, quartered
1 thin slice stale bread, without crusts
1 garlic clove, finely chopped
salt and freshly ground black pepper
1¼ tablespoons red wine vinegar
3 tablespoons olive oil
flat parsley leaves, if available, or lettuce leaves

Hard-cook the eggs 12 minutes, drain and immediately cover with cold water to stop the yolks from graying. Turn the tuna into a wide bowl and shred it with a fork. Quarter the sweet peppers and scrupulously remove all the ribs inside. Cut into long thin shreds (double-matchstick width) and then into neat dice. With a sharp knife take out the insides of the tomatoes. Slice and then dice the quarters. Chop the hard egg whites the same size (reserve the yolks), mix everything together and chill.

Soak the bread in water, then squeeze out. Work the garlic to a paste with the salt and hard-cooked egg yolks in a small blender. Add the bread, vinegar and pepper and purée again. Work in the oil and purée to a smooth cream. Dress the salad 30 minutes before serving, tossing it gently, and pile on individual salad plates. A flurry of single flat parsley leaves makes a pretty garnish, or a curly lettuce leaf.

ENSALADILLA

"LITTLE" OR "RUSSIAN" SALAD

This little salad is peculiarly suited to Spain. It probably dates back to the Napoleonic wars, when so many Frenchmen took up residence in Spain, at a time when food "in the Russian style" was all the rage in Paris. This salad is a regular in *tapas* bars.

For a cold lunch dish, serve with tuna-stuffed eggs – another Spanish invention. I also have a modern recipe from Algeciras, which adds a little curry paste to the mayonnaise and ½ pound of peeled cooked shrimp to the salad ingredients.

SERVES 4

1¼ lb potatoes, each about 2 oz
1 large carrot, in big dice
3 tablespoons peas
1 sweet green pepper, stem, seeds and ribs removed
salt and pepper
3 tablespoons mild Spanish onion, chopped to ½ pea size
16 oz canned artichoke hearts, quartered
1½ tablespoons capers
8 midget gherkins, chopped
8 ripe olives, 3 strips cut from around each pit
1 canned pimiento

MAYONNAISE
2 extra-large egg yolks
2 – 3 tablespoons lemon juice
pinch of salt
1¼ cups Spanish or "pure" olive oil
1 – 2 tablespoons white wine or warm water

Choose egg-sized potatoes and boil them in their skins (which tastes better) in salted water 20 – 25 minutes. If they are larger than this, or peeled, the outside crumbles or the flesh gets too wet to make a good salad. Cool, then skin, the potatoes; slice them, then chop to the size of bread cubes. Cook the carrot and peas. Cut the sweet pepper into strips and dice them. Mix everything together, seasoning well. Fold in the onion, artichokes, capers and gherkins.

Make the mayonnaise. Put the egg yolks into a bowl with 2 teaspoons of lemon juice or the salt and beat well. A hand-held electric beater is easiest to use and will warm up yolks taken directly from the refriger-

ator. Gentle warmth is the key to making an emulsion and so to easy mayonnaise. Spanish kitchens are always warm, but in an air-conditioned one, stand the measuring cup of olive oil in a pan of hot water.

Add about 2 teaspoons of oil at first, making sure it is blended before proceeding. Add a little oil at a time, beating in each batch. Finally, taste and add seasoning. The mayonnaise will be a thick yellow butter, which can then be diluted with warm water, or in this case wine, to make the familiar cream for coating.

Pour the mayonnaise over the vegetables and toss

MARKET IN SAN SEBASTIAN *Sun-colored Mediterranean vegetables like tomatoes and sweet peppers are by no means used exclusively in Spanish dishes – glossy leaved greens are equally valued.*

gently. Turn into a 1½-quart capacity loaf pan (pressing gently into the corners) or a gratin dish, and chill until needed. Work around the sides of the pan with a narrow metal spatula before unmolding. If you wish, more mayonnaise can be spread on the outside – make a 3-egg quantity for this. Decorate with crisscross strips of pimiento enclosing ripe olives.

FISH AND
SHELLFISH

*With Spain's thousands of miles of coastline
and inland mountain streams, it is no
surprise that the Spaniards' love of fish and
shellfish knows no bounds.*

VIEIRAS DE SANTIAGO *left (p 91)*, MERLUZA CON SALSA
VERDE *right (p 83)*.

WITH COASTS ON TWO OCEANS, one brisk and cold, the other lazy and warm, the variety of Spanish fish and shellfish is enormous. Spain also has fast mountain streams teaming with salmon and trout. Eating fish and shellfish is a national passion.

The barbecue may just be a stick in the ground piercing a row of sardines by a beach fire, for the cooking in Spain is simple, but always appropriate. Plain frying, with a little lemon juice squeezed over afterward, shows off varieties of fish hardly known outside the country. Skill at deep frying seems to be universal – golden crispness on the outside is the result, without a trace of oil. These traditional methods have been developed to show off simple flavors: like salmon, soaked in lemon, salt and milk, then grilled over charcoal, or brown trout, cooked in white wine, or wrapped in or stuffed with raw ham.

There are also the great soup-stews, encrusted with shellfish. On the north coast *caldeirada de pescado* throws together a variety of clawed and shelled creatures, with great chunks of fish, and the Catalan coast has the splendors of *zarzuela* and a similar, tomatoless dish called *suquet* or *susquet*.

Even inland villages have markets with wet piles of shimmering silver fish like sardines, a bewildering choice from the sea. The charmingly-named *salmonetes*, or red mullet, grilled without cleaning, are piled next to small brown sole, looking like lost shoes. Shark flesh lies skinned on the fish counters, pink and defenseless like great meat bones, destined to end up in stews. Steaks of swordfish, *pez espáda*, with its black plastic-like skin, are good for grilling.

The favorite of so many Spaniards is *merluza*, hake, loved for its delicate flavor and flaky texture, though hake recipes can be cooked with whiting, cod or haddock. Another famous Mediterranean fish is the *mero*, a grouper, and a proverb says that the best things to eat are "the lamb from the mountain and the *mero* from the sea." I suspect the Spaniards taught the rest of Europe to eat monkfish, and you can see great saddles in the Boqueria market in Barcelona, ready for roasting.

Traditionally the Basques have been the Atlantic fishermen, adding another fish – cod – to the Spanish repertoire, since it is unknown in the Mediterranean.

The Basque specialty is *bacalao*, salt cod, with the local sweet peppers, and *bacalao* is still extremely popular throughout the country, especially during Holy Week. The coming of frozen fish has made no dent upon what was, at one time, just a convenience food.

The diversity of the shellfish is amazing. Spain has many sorts of shrimp, each with their own names. These are cooked and eaten simply, like the *gambas de Palomos*, which are boiled for exactly three minutes, then placed on ice to arrest further cooking. *Langostino* is one of the bigger shrimp, though its name is deceptively close to the French *langoustine*, which is called *cigala* in Spain. This latter is a clawed saltwater crayfish, and is unusual in being pink and white even when alive at the market. *Langosta*, the spiny rock-lobster, is valued for the sweet meat which is all in the tail, and is normally boiled and served plain with mayonnaise.

The star of the north coast is *centolla*, the spider crab. It is stronger and sweeter than the clawed crab, but there is less meat, so this is normally mixed with hake, then stuffed back into its shell.

Both coasts have mussels in plenty and there are sea dates, sea urchins in their hedgehog shells and a huge selection of tiny clams, each with local names. *Navajas* are razor shells, and come from the market bundled with string, an occasional white tongue lapping out of a brown end. And strangest of all are barnacles called *percebes*, which stand from the rock like miniature black bear's claws, complete with white fingernails.

The *concha fina*, "finest shell," of the south coast is a big Venus shell. The best place to eat these in is one of the sherry bars of Malaga, where an old man sits all day at the task of opening them. Here the sherry barrels are stacked to the roof, each with its grape scrawled across the butt. You may choose from this one, then that, while the huge shells are opened before you, a glory of scarlet and orange roes.

Squid are extremely popular, the more so as freezing does not spoil them. Fried rings of *calamares* are ubiquitous, but on the northern, Cantabrian coast, squid fried in bread crumbs are sold as *rabas*. Cuttlefish is normally stewed. The rich sweetness of its black ink is featured in the exotic *sepia en su tinto* in the north and in the east coast rice dish, *arroz negro*.

MERLUZA CON SALSA VERDE

HAKE WITH GREEN SAUCE

The green wine-and-parsley sauce of this famous Santander casserole is one of the nicest complements to the delicate flavor of hake. It is often served in individual casseroles and the sauce, which may be of soup proportions, may well include lots of fishy extras. Clams are traditional, and any shellfish that traps a little seawater inside its shell. Another version includes the Basque specialty *kokotxas*, or hake cheeks, a tiny "oyster" of sweet flesh from beyond the fish's eye.

Doña Plácida de Larrea of Bilbao wrote to a friend in 1723, describing the dish, and added that her husband liked a light, sweetish white wine with it. Marqués de Cáceres make a light white Rioja that is the best wine in the new fresh, fruity, style of white Riojas, none of which taste of oak casks, as they are not aged in wood.

SERVES 4

2 tablespoons butter
2 tablespoons olive oil
1 onion, finely chopped
2 garlic cloves, finely chopped
4 pieces of hake or whiting fillet, about 6 oz each
salt and freshly ground black pepper
2 tablespoons flour
1½ cups fish stock
¾ cup dry white wine, preferably Rioja
½ lb littleneck clams, rinsed
½ lb mussels, cleaned (see page 96)
1½ cups shelled peas, cooked if fresh
6 tablespoons chopped parsley

Heat the butter and oil in a flameproof casserole into which all the fish will fit comfortably, and fry the onion gently until soft, adding the garlic near the end. Season the fish pieces and flour lightly. Push the onion to the sides of the pan and add the fish, skin side up. Cook them slowly, turning them over once, until light golden.

Add the fish stock and white wine and bring to the simmering point. Add the shellfish and, when the shells open, the peas, and simmer 5 minutes. Stir in the parsley and check the seasoning. Serve in soup plates.

ESQUEIXADA

CATALAN SALT COD AND SWEET PEPPER SALAD

Aficionados will tell you that *bacalao*, salt cod, is one of the great acquired tastes – like caviar or truffles. And this salad from L'Empordà, the Costa Brava region, will be a revelation to anyone who has not eaten dried cod before, and doesn't quite like the sound of it. The fish is translucent and mild, pickled by the vinaigrette, rather than cooked. The name of the dish comes from the Catalan verb "to shred."

SERVES 4–6

½ lb thick salt cod, soaked 48 hours
(see page 10)
¼ small onion, sliced very finely
3 tablespoons virgin olive oil
1 tablespoon red wine vinegar
freshly ground black pepper
2 sweet red peppers, stems and seeds removed
2 fat ripe tomatoes, without skin
12–18 small ripe olives for garnish

Drain the cod and then blot well with paper towels. If the flesh is chunky, cut it into strips and press gently in paper towels to remove the last water. Discard the skin, bones and any discolored flesh and remove all membrane.

Shred the cod finely with your fingers – the result looks more like white mushrooms than fish. Add some slivered onion – the equivalent of 1½ tablespoons. Combine the oil and vinegar and pour over. Sprinkle with pepper, toss and let marinate 2–3 hours in a cool place.

Slice the sweet peppers not much bigger than matchsticks and pour boiling water over them, to soften them a little. After 10 minutes, drain and dry on paper towels. Quarter the tomatoes and remove the inside with a knife. Slice the flesh neatly. Stir the fish and all the salad ingredients together gently. Arrange on side plates and garnish with ripe olives.

FRITOS DE PESCADO A LA MALAGUEÑA

MIXED FRIED FISH, MALAGA STYLE

Andalusia is sometimes called *zona de los fritos*: Cadiz, Malaga and the province of Murcia are all known for their superb fried fish. The elegant city of Malaga, which has survived the influx of tourists better than some others on the coast, is known for this sophisticated dish, with its different colors and textures. For four people, fry only three types of fish, omitting one variety of white fish and the squid.

SERVES 6

½ lb sole fillets
½ lb hake, whiting, cod or haddock fillet
3 × 6 oz red mullet (goatfish)
½ lb fresh anchovies, small sardines or whitebait (the fry of herring or silverside)
flour for dusting
⅔–¾ cup olive oil for frying
½ lb small squid, cleaned (see page 95)
2 lemons, cut in wedges
sprigs of flat parsley for garnish
salt and freshly ground black pepper

Skin the sole fillets by laying them skin side down and running a sharp knife between the skin and the flesh. Cut the sole into broad strips and the hake into chunks. Keep each type of fish in a separate pile.

Run a knife the wrong way along the mullet to remove all the sequinlike scales, then cut off the head and tail and gut the fish. Open them up and remove the backbones, pulling carefully at any bones around the stomach vent. Halve lengthwise along the back, then cut each fillet into three. Clean and split the anchovies or sardines (see page 24): whitebait can be used whole.

When ready to cook, season and flour all the fish. Heat plenty of oil, preferably in several skillets, and fry the fish, starting with the thickest and keeping the types separate. Turn them carefully until nicely cooked on each side and remove to drain on paper towels. A big *paella* pan or round serving dish is best for serving. Put in all the fish, each in a group, dividing each section from the next with lemon wedges, one turned up, the rest turned down. Put several parsley sprigs in the middle and serve immediately.

A good choice of white wine would be the long-established Marqués de Riscal, from Rueda. In a wire-covered bottle, originally intended to prevent tampering with the contents, it is made from one of the few Spanish grapes of character, Verdejo.

CARABINEROS CON WHISKEY

LARGE SHRIMP WITH WHISKEY

Their brilliant color earns these scarlet "guardsmen" their military name. This and their sheer size – up to 9 inches long – command respect, but in fact their flavor is slightly less good than that of other large shrimp. Brandy, rum and, in modern times, imported whiskey, are therefore used to improve this. With good-quality shrimp the dish will be even better.

SERVES 4

3–4 tablespoons olive oil
1 onion, finely chopped
½ lb ripe tomatoes, without skin or seeds, or 1 cup canned tomatoes, with juice
2 lb jumbo or large shrimp, shelled
¾ teaspoon salt
¼ cup Scotch whiskey

Heat 2 tablespoons of oil in a skillet and add the onion, cooking it slowly until softened. Add the chopped tomato and cook until it is reduced to a sauce. Push the sauce to the edges of the pan, add 1–2 tablespoons more oil and put in the peeled shrimp. Cook about 4 minutes, depending on size, stirring occasionally, and sprinkle with salt.

Warm the whiskey in a ladle, set light to it and pour it over the shrimp. Stir the shrimp into the sauce and serve them at once.

PIXIN A LA ASTURIANA

MONKFISH IN APPLE AND CIDER SAUCE

Cider is firmly entrenched on the north coast of Spain: indeed, the Basques claim to have invented it. It is a strong alcoholic drink in Spain, unlike ordinary American cider. If you cannot get hard (alcoholic) cider, you can use ordinary cider, but add a good shot of applejack. *Pixin* is the local Asturian name for monkfish, called *rape* elsewhere in Spain. It's one of the fish most solidly incorporated into Spanish cuisine, and its shellfishlike taste has become fashionable elsewhere.

SERVES 4

1 onion, chopped
⅓ cup olive oil
2 garlic cloves, finely chopped
1 ripe tomato, without skin or seeds, diced
pinch of cayenne
2 sweet apples (optionally 4)
1 cup dry hard cider
1 teaspoon tomato paste
1 lb potatoes, diced to the size of bread cubes
1½ lb monkfish on the bone
1 tablespoon lemon juice
salt and freshly ground black pepper
about 2 tablespoons flour
½ lb littleneck clams, rinsed

Fry the onion in 2 tablespoons of oil in a saucepan. As it softens, add the garlic. Add the tomato flesh, cayenne and cored, chopped apples. Stir in the cider and cook 15 minutes. Check the seasonings, adding the tomato paste if the tomato was not large or ripe enough, and purée everything in a blender. Return to the pan. Heat the oven to 350° F.

Heat ¼ cup of oil over medium-high heat in a skillet and fry the potatoes, tossing them regularly. Reserve in the oven in an earthenware casserole or serving dish.

Remove the gray skin from the monkfish and also the less noticeable skin inside the belly cavity. Take the fish off the bone and portion it. Sprinkle the fish with lemon juice and season and flour it lightly. Add 2 more tablespoons of oil to the skillet and fry the fish, turning, until golden. Transfer to the dish containing the potatoes. Reserve a quarter of the potatoes and fit the rest between the fish portions in the dish.

Reheat the sauce, adding the clams (which will open), and pour over the fish. Garnish with the reserved potatoes. Give the dish 10 minutes in the oven for the flavors to blend. Fried apple rings also make a good garnish. Spanish cider is rarely exported, so drink your own to accompany it.

TILED KITCHEN *Since the 13th century, ceramics, particularly* azulejos, *glazed tiles, have been used in decoration.*

MARMITAKO

MACKEREL AND SWEET RED PEPPER STEW

A shipboard stew, eaten by Basque fishermen, *marmitako* is often made with tuna, but the dish is also a good way of eating the cheaper mackerel. Its name comes from the pot used for cooking it, better known to us by the French name of *marmite*.

Dry wine is needed in the recipe to balance the rich, sweet, piquant peppers and oily fish. Dry hard cider could also be used (and drunk with it). If, however, you don't want to open a bottle, use instead the juice of 3 lemons or, more unconventionally, 2 limes. It's my belief the tomatoes are a recent addition, and that this is in fact the famous fish sauce that appears in Basque recipes *a la vizcaina*, most notably for *bacalao*, or salt cod. Older recipes for *marmitako* talk of soaking the peppers in water for 24 hours and they were originally the only vegetable in the sauce.

SERVES 4 – 5

3 large sweet red peppers
¼ cup olive oil
1 onion, chopped
2 garlic cloves, finely chopped
2 – 3 small mackerel (about 2 lb before cleaning), filleted (or 1¼ lb tuna)
salt and freshly ground black pepper
⅔ cup dry white wine
1 small dried chili pepper, seeded and chopped
16 oz canned tomatoes, with juice
1 lb potatoes, in small cubes
2 teaspoons paprika
2 tablespoons chopped parsley

Quarter and seed the sweet peppers, then pour about 7 cups of boiling water over them and let soak and soften 2 – 3 hours. Heat the oil in a large shallow flameproof casserole, big enough to take the fish. Fry the chopped onion gently, adding the garlic when it is nearly soft.

Cut each mackerel fillet into 3 or 4 pieces and season them well. Push the onion to the sides of the casserole, put in the fish and fry it on both sides.

Add the wine to the casserole with the pieces of dried chili pepper. Add the pulped tomatoes – on board ship this is done by squeezing each one in the hand and letting it run out through the fingers into the sauce. On dry land you can pulse them briefly in a food processor. Distribute the potato cubes over the top and sprinkle them with paprika and more salt and pepper.

Drain the sweet peppers, saving the liquid, then shred them (or process them briefly) and add to the pan with enough of the soaking liquid to cover the potatoes well. Cook about 20 minutes, or until the potatoes are well done and the liquid somewhat reduced. Check the seasonings, stir in the chopped parsley, and serve the stew in soup bowls.

TRUCHAS CON SALSA ROMESCO

MOUNTAIN TROUT WITH PIQUANT ALMOND SAUCE

Thickened with hazelnuts and almonds combined with bread, this is one of the oldest ways of making sauce in Europe – a mountain sauce, in a country where hills face the coast at almost every turn. It's my belief that it was previously seasoned with black pepper, of which the Catalonians are extraordinarily fond. The red *romesco* pepper which now gives its name to the sauce was then introduced – along with the tomato – in the 16th century, resulting in a more successful version of the same peppery taste.

Called a *ñora* pepper in other parts of Spain, the *romesco* is spicy without really being hot. For those with access to Mexican stores, Colman Andrews, in *Catalan Cuisine*, suggests substituting ½ canned *jalapeño* pepper, plus 3 dried *ancho* peppers. I also recommend a little *jalapeño* ketchup.

Romesco makes an interesting accompaniment for roast chicken or a cold Christmas Eve salmon, but is most frequently served with fried fish. The sauce may then include the fried fish livers – often an unwanted gift from whole fish.

Start the sauce by toasting the nuts in a low oven – about 300° F – for 20 minutes, until very lightly browned. Heat 4 tablespoons of oil in a skillet, frying the garlic while it heats; remove and reserve the garlic, then fry the bread briskly on both sides and reserve it.

Add 2 more tablespoons of oil to the skillet, then the chopped tomatoes and the cayenne or *jalapeño* pepper, stirring until much reduced. Grind the nuts in a blender, then add the bread and garlic and pulverize them with the vinegar and sherry to make a *picada* – a piquant last-minute addition to the sauce. Stir this into the sauce. If you wish, the whole sauce can be blended once more to a pink "mayonnaise," adding a few extra tablespoonfuls of oil.

Heat the broiler. Wash the trout inside and out and salt and pepper them. Brush them with the butter and oil and broil 5–7 minutes on each side, turning once. Serve on hot plates, with the sauce, accompanied by an aristocratic white Rioja in the old style, such as the *blanco reserva* from Marqués de Murrieta, which has some lemon acidity as well as an oakiness from the casks in which it is matured.

SERVES 4

4 trout, each ½ – ¾ lb, cleaned
salt and freshly ground black pepper
2 tablespoons melted butter
2 tablespoons olive oil

SALSA ROMESCO

25 shelled almonds, blanched
25 shelled hazelnuts, blanched
6 tablespoons olive oil
2 garlic cloves, finely chopped
1 slice of day-old bread
½ lb ripe tomatoes, without skin or seeds, or 1 cup canned tomatoes, with juice
2 teaspoons red wine vinegar
¼ cup fino sherry
pinch of cayenne or ½-inch piece of canned jalapeño pepper, seeded

BACALAO EN SAMFAINA

SALT COD IN MIXED VEGETABLE SAUCE

The Basques cook *bacalao* with onions and the local peppers, which are bright red, sweet and a good deal more spicy than sweet bell peppers. The result is called *bacalao a la vizcaina*, Spain's most famous salt cod dish.

When the dish is made outside the Basque country, however, the sauce often includes a great deal of tomato – perhaps to compensate for the lack of those famous peppers. I have therefore chosen a popular salt cod recipe with tomato sauce as its base, though lots of other vegetables are included, too.

Samfaina is one of Spain's best-known sauces. A vegetable dish in its own right when served by itself or with pork chops, it is often cooked with chicken.

VILLAGE IN THE PYRENEES *In spite of the better roads that have been built in the Pyrenees, access to many hamlets and villages remains difficult and here life – and cooking methods – have changed little over the centuries.*

SERVES 4

1 lb thick salt cod, soaked overnight
(see page 10)
about 4–5 tablespoons olive oil

SAMFAINA

½ lb eggplant, without stem or skin
2 tablespoons olive oil
1 large onion, chopped
¼ lb smoked ham (optional)
2 garlic cloves, finely chopped
1½ lb ripe tomatoes, without skin or seeds, or 3 cups
canned tomatoes, with juice
2 sweet red peppers, seeded and cut in squares
¾ cup dry white wine
1 bay leaf
1 large zucchini, cubed with the skin on
salt and freshly ground black pepper

Cube the eggplant, sprinkle with salt and let stand in a colander 30 minutes. Remove the skin and all the bones from the salt cod, discarding any discolored flesh. Cut the fish into "fingers," following the natural shape, and blot well with paper towels.

Start the *samfaina*. Heat the oil in a flameproof casserole big enough to take all the ingredients. Fry the onion and ham, if using, over medium heat until the onion colors, then add the garlic. Add the tomato, sweet peppers, wine and bay leaf and simmer gently, stirring occasionally, until the tomato has disintegrated into a sauce.

Meanwhile, put 4–5 tablespoons of oil in a skillet and fry the fish pieces on both sides until well colored and golden, then remove from the pan and add to the tomato sauce.

Rinse the salt off the eggplant and pat dry with paper towels. Add more oil to the skillet if needed and fry the eggplant and zucchini cubes gently, turning them occasionally. When they are golden, add to the tomato sauce and fish and simmer, covered, 15 minutes: a little water may be needed. Check the seasonings and serve.

RAPE CON MAHONESA
Y ENSALADA DE ARROZ

COLD MONKFISH IN MAYONNAISE
WITH RICE SALAD

The Duc de Richelieu brought mayonnaise back to France after capturing the port of Mahon in Menorca in 1756. Did his chef invent it there, with local ingredients, or did he discover a Spanish invention? The Spaniards naturally favor a spelling of the sauce which emphasizes their role and Elizabeth David lends support to a local origin, in *French Provincial Cookery*: "It certainly seems likely that by the 1750s the sauce was already known in Spain and Provence."

In April and May, when blood oranges are in season, I add orange juice, cream and cayenne to make pink mayonnaise for shellfish. But I was amused to find that even Michelin-starred chefs use a dab of ketchup for the rest of the year. This is a really wonderful sauce for boiled lobster, but is more often eaten with rounds of monkfish, which superficially resemble lobster, or a combination of fish such as hake or whiting and shrimp.

SERVES 4

1½ lb monkfish on the bone
¾ cup dry white wine
dusting of paprika

RICE SALAD
1¼ cups long-grain rice
1 sweet green pepper, stem and seeds removed
1 lb ripe tomatoes, without skin or seeds
¼ cup olive oil
2 tablespoons wine vinegar
1 garlic clove, finely chopped
½ teaspoon Dijon-style mustard
pinch of sugar
¼ teaspoon salt
freshly ground black pepper

PINK MAYONNAISE
½ cup thick mayonnaise (see page 78)
2 tablespoons orange juice
1 tablespoon ketchup
1 tablespoon thick cream (optional)

Sprinkle the rice into plenty of boiling salted water, stir once and simmer 15 minutes. Drain in a sieve, running cold water through it to remove starch, then bounce 2–3 times to drain the rice again. Spread it out on paper towels to dry.

Cut down on either side of the monkfish bone and remove it. Peel away all skin, including the white belly skin, and lay the fish fillets head to tail in a small oval pan or flameproof casserole. Cover with white wine and bring gently to the simmering point. Cook 8 minutes, then drain and cool.

Cut out the ribs from the sweet pepper, then slice and cut into small dice. Quarter the tomatoes, cut out the insides, then dice. Make a dressing from the remaining salad ingredients, then season the rice and stir in the sweet peppers and dressing. Add the tomatoes only at the last moment, as they may ooze juice into the rice.

Trim any loose bits off the fish (chopping them into the rice) and then cut each fillet into 8 neat rounds. Mix the flavorings into the mayonnaise – the cream can be whipped if it is thin. Make a rice bed on a serving dish and arrange the monkfish on top, coating each piece with mayonnaise. Sprinkle the fish very lightly with paprika. This is an easy summer dish, so drink with it an easy summer white wine. Fresh, dry and a little lemony, Torres Viña Sol is not aged and is the best of the white wines made exclusively from Parellada, the Spanish grape, but in the new French style.

VIEIRAS DE SANTIAGO

ST. JAMES'S BAKED SCALLOPS

Scallops in Galicia are huge – often monster 8-year-olds, so a single one makes a portion. The creamy orange coral curls around the firmer white in late summer, rather like a poached egg in reverse. Every restaurant in the old town of Santiago seems to offer this dish on St. James's Day: a pleasant variation on the white wine and mushroom *coquilles St. Jacques*.

SERVES 4

1 lb sea scallops off the shell or, preferably, 2–3
good-sized sea scallops on the shell per person
1 tablespoon butter
3 tablespoons oil
¼ cup aguardiente, Fundador or another Spanish
brandy
1 onion, finely chopped
3 garlic cloves, finely chopped
½ lb ripe tomatoes, without skin or seeds, or ¾ cup
canned tomatoes, with juice
1 teaspoon paprika
pinch of cayenne or ½ small dried chili pepper, without
seeds, chopped
½ cup white wine or good fish stock
salt and freshly ground black pepper
2–3 tablespoons fine bread crumbs
1 tablespoon finely chopped parsley

WINDOW IN GRANADA *Stucco decoration adds a splash of color.*

ZARZUELA (overleaf) *(p 94)*.

If buying scallops on the shell, also ask for the curved, deep upper shell. To clean the scallops, hold a knife flat against the shell and cut the flesh free, then remove the ring of gristle that often surrounds the white. Separate large corals, which take only seconds to cook, from the white. Shelled scallops may need cleaning by pulling away any dark gut at the root of the coral, but more often they are coralless.

Heat the butter with 1 tablespoon of oil and quickly fry the white parts of the scallops 2 minutes on each side. The corals are then added and just flipped in the hot butter. Shelled or thawed frozen scallops tend to make a lot of liquid, so remove them when cooked and boil this off. Warm the *aguardiente* or brandy, flame it and pour over the scallops. Spoon them into the upper shells or small heatproof dishes.

Add 2 tablespoons of oil and fry the onion gently until soft, adding the garlic toward the end. Add the chopped tomato, paprika and cayenne or chili pepper and cook to reduce. Moisten with the wine or fish stock, season and spoon over the scallops. Mix the bread crumbs and parsley together and sprinkle thinly over the top. Heat through for 2–3 minutes under the broiler and serve immediately.

Tomato and brandy make this a rich dish and if it is an appetizer, choose a dry *fino* or *amontillado* sherry to accompany it. If the scallops are a main course, partner them with an oaky white Rioja *reserva*, like the classic Marqués de Murrieta.

ZARZUELA

A MEDLEY OF FISH

A *zarzuela* is a theatrical performance, a combination of light opera and witty, satirical comedy. It took its name from the Zarzuela, the king's informal home in Madrid. This Catalan dish evokes the operetta, for it is another wonderful mixture – this time of tastes and colors, shapes and textures – and the flaming alcohol poured over it makes its own *coup de théâtre*.

To put on the performance, the various acts need a little planning. It's a 3-pan job (4 if your casserole is not table-worthy), but it is not difficult to do. Look for an anise-scented alcohol: colorless *aguardiente* is ideal. I also like *pacharán*, which is like an anise-scented brandy, made from sloes and normally drunk on the rocks. Zoco is the best-known brand and flames beautifully. It is rather like a brown, sweeter version of Pernod. However, some exported *pacharáns* are lower in alcohol and this has to be boiled off before it is poured over.

The dish will serve six people as an appetizer, four as a main course.

SERVES 4

2½ *cups good fish stock*
⅓ *cup* fino *sherry*
2 *bay leaves, crumbled*
½ *lb mussels, cleaned (see page 96)*
½ *lb littleneck clams (or extra mussels), rinsed*
5 *tablespoons olive oil*
1 *onion, chopped*
1 *garlic clove, finely chopped*
3 *tablespoons chopped parsley*
¾ *lb ripe tomatoes, without skin or seeds, or* 1½ *cups canned tomatoes, with juice*
¾ *lb white fish fillets, in 4 portions*
salt and freshly ground black pepper
4 *small squid, cleaned (see page 95)*
½ *cup Pernod, Spanish brandy or* pacharán
10 *saffron strands*
4 *langoustines or jumbo shrimp*
¼ *lb medium-sized shrimp in the shell*
¼ *lb small shrimp*

Heat the stock with the sherry and bay leaves in a saucepan and put in the mussels. Cover and cook a couple of minutes until they open. Remove the mussels and add the clams. Remove the empty top shells from both shellfish. Strain the stock. Pour a little over the saffron in a cup, and reserve the remaining stock.

Start the sauce base. Heat 2 tablespoons of oil in a large flameproof casserole, big enough to take all the shellfish. Fry the onion gently until soft, adding the garlic, then the parsley toward the end. Add the chopped tomatoes and let them reduce to a sauce.

Heat 3 tablespoons of oil in a skillet. Season the fish pieces and then fry over medium heat, turning once, until light golden. Add the squid rings and tentacles and fry briefly. Heat the Pernod, brandy or *pacharán* in a ladle and, standing well back, set it alight and spoon over the fish until the flames die down. Or boil the *pacharán*, then pour over.

Stir the saffron mixture and stock into the casserole. Bring to the simmering point, then add the *langoustines* and any raw shrimp. Cook them 5 minutes, then add cooked shrimp. Fit the fish pieces and juices into the casserole, with the squid, then add the clams and mussels. Simmer gently a couple of minutes, then serve in soup plates.

Put out plenty of paper napkins, nutcrackers and spare plates for the shells. To eat *langoustines*, first pull off the head and suck the inside. There may be some meat inside big claws, so these are worth cracking, but there is nothing in the legs. Hold the body with finger and thumb on either side and press together to snap the stomach shell. Then peel the legs up over the back, like a shrimp to remove the shell. Pinch the tail hard to release the vacuum, then pull the body out of the remaining shell.

Torres Gran Viña Sol "Green Label" is a rich white wine with enough character to stand up well to the assortment of flavors. It contains some Sauvignon grapes and has a hint of oak casks about it.

SEPIA GUISADA CON ALBÓNDIGAS Y GUISANTES

CUTTLEFISH WITH MEATBALLS AND PEAS

The Catalans invented "surf and turf" to eke out one expensive ingredient with another cheap one – originally the festive chicken with the free lobster. The same idea is behind this dish from L'Empordà, between Barcelona and the French frontier. It could be nicknamed "poor man's veal," for it's rather like eating veal served two different ways.

Buy a large cuttlefish if you can, because its flesh is thicker and sweeter than squid, or one of the big squid fished in northern waters. If using small squid, keep the tentacles for a pretty salad and use only the bodies in this recipe.

SERVES 4

1½ lb big cuttlefish or squid
3 tablespoons olive oil
1 slice of stale bread
1 onion, chopped
6 garlic cloves, finely chopped
3 tablespoons finely chopped parsley
1 tablespoon flour
¼ lb ripe tomatoes, without skin or seeds
1¼ cups meat or chicken stock
salt and freshly ground black pepper
½ cup dry white wine
2⅔ cups shelled peas, fresh or frozen

MEATBALLS

2 slices of stale bread
¼ cup dry white wine
½ lb lean ground pork
½ lb ground beef
2 tablespoons finely chopped onion
1 tablespoon finely chopped parsley
freshly grated nutmeg
½ teaspoon coarse salt
freshly ground black pepper
1 extra-large egg, beaten, for coating
flour for coating
3 tablespoons olive oil, for frying

To clean squid, grip the tentacles and use them to pull out the insides. Cut across above the eyes and discard everything below. Large squid (and cuttlefish) have a mouthpiece in the center of the tentacles which can be popped backward like a button. Flex the body gently and the spinal structure, like transparent plastic, will pop out. Cuttlefish are very similar, except the body looks like a plump coin purse with a frill around it, instead of a rocket with fins. Slit the body up both sides and remove the cuttle bone. Wash squid and cuttlefish well inside under running water. Rub off the skin with salt-coated hands and wash again. Cut the body into squares the size of large postage stamps and the tentacles of large shellfish into short lengths.

Make the sauce in a deep flameproof casserole without too big a base. Heat the oil, fry the bread over high heat till golden and remove to a blender. Fry the onion gently until it starts to soften, then add the garlic and parsley. Add to the blender and reduce everything to a purée – this is the *picada*.

Sprinkle the flour into the casserole (more oil may be needed) and cook over medium-high heat until it turns brown. This is important to give the sauce its dark meaty taste, but be careful that it does not burn. Add the chopped tomatoes and stock and simmer to reduce. Traditionally the *picada* is added to thicken the sauce and then the whole thing is sieved. The easier way, however, is to add the contents of the casserole to the blender and purée everything once more. Return the sauce to the casserole, add the prepared shellfish and season with salt and pepper. Simmer 15 minutes, or 30 minutes if using frozen peas.

Make the meatballs. Sprinkle the bread with wine, then squeeze it out lightly and combine all the ingredients, seasoning well. Make large marble-sized balls and roll them in beaten egg. Transfer them to a plate covered with plenty of flour and shake it to and fro until the balls are coated. Heat 3 tablespoons of oil in a skillet and fry the balls over high heat, shaking frequently so they color and crisp on all sides.

Add the wine and peas to the casserole and cook till the peas are tender (20 minutes for fresh peas, 5 for frozen). Slip the meatballs into the sauce, bring back to the simmering point and give them a minute or so in the sauce. Long-grain rice makes a good partner.

MEJILLONES A LA MARINERA

SAILORS' SPICY MUSSELS

The Galician seaboard not only provides Spain with over a quarter of its national fish catch, but also gives the region the damp, misty weather that makes warming dishes particularly appreciated in its cooking.

Comforting and spicy on a cold day, I first ate these mussels in blustery weather at Muros, a small port on the way to the Atlantic outpost of Cape Finisterre – once considered the outpost of the world.

SERVES 4

3 lb large mussels
½ cup dry white wine
1 small onion, chopped
1½ tablespoons olive oil
1 garlic clove, finely chopped
1 tablespoon flour
½ bay leaf, crumbled
1 teaspoon tomato paste
½ teaspoon paprika
tiny pinch of cayenne or mild chili powder
salt
1 teaspoon lemon juice

MENDING NETS IN LEVANT PORT *As well as the cooler Atlantic ports, Spain has all the variety of the warm Mediterranean to choose from, making it nothing short of a fish lover's heaven.*

Cover the mussels in cold water and scrub the shells, discarding any that are smashed or do not shut when touched. Pull off all "beards." Do not clean them too far ahead, as this removes their life support system and they die.

Heat the wine in a saucepan with a lid and add the mussels in 3–4 batches. Cook briefly, covered, and remove them when they open, discarding any that remain shut. Reserve the liquid. Remove the top shell and arrange the biggest mussels in an ovenproof dish. Use a loose shell to cut the smaller mussels free and put 2 mussels in each shell.

For the sauce, fry the onion in the oil in a small pan, adding the garlic and then the flour when the onion softens. Cook briefly. Meanwhile, boil the mussel liquid down to about ¾ cup, then add it to the pan with the bay leaf. Bring to the simmering point, taste and add the tomato paste, paprika, cayenne and a little salt and lemon juice, as needed. Strain the sauce, then pour it over the mussels and heat them briefly (5 minutes under the broiler or in a moderate oven). As the mussels are distinctly spicy, you can serve Spain's best-known lager, San Miguel, which has plenty of flavor of its own, would make a good thirst-quencher.

PULPO A LA FERIA

FESTIVE SPICED OCTOPUS SALAD

Octopus is very popular in the north of Spain and on St. James's Day octopuses stand on all the bars in Santiago, purple-red but unthreatening. They look like great pincushions, or pink wigs standing propped ready-for-use on hat stands, a mass of pink rings curling away on all sides. Beside each one there is invariably a great stack of wooden plates, on which they are served.

It's difficult to decide whether the flesh tastes more like rabbit, chicken or tuna; it is white and firm, and Spanish cooks add a few bottle corks to the water when cooking, to make it more tender. This appears to work and is easier than tenderizing it by thumping it.

SERVES 4–6

1¾–2 lb octopus
coarse salt
1 large onion
6 tablespoons olive oil
1 garlic clove, finely chopped
1 teaspoon paprika
*2 pinches of cayenne or a little
mild chili powder*
freshly ground pepper
flat parsley leaves for garnish

Octopus is always displayed upside-down and inside out. To clean it, stretch out the tentacles and the bag which is the head. Make a cut around the head above the eyes and pull gently to remove the organs inside the head. Discard these, with the ink sac. Turn the body inside out and wash thoroughly. Work around the beak in the mouth with a knife and cut this out, too.

Dip your hands in coarse salt and rub down the tentacles to remove all the skin. This is tougher than the membrane on squid, and comes away with a little flesh on the inside. Each sucker contains a little ring and big ones will need popping out with finger and

RETURNING FROM MARKET *Supreme freshness in fish is highly prized and a fish that a short time ago was swimming in the sea may in a matter of hours have been caught, bought from the market and simply prepared, in just the way to bring out its natural flavors.*

thumb, like a pop-it button.

In Spain octopus is beaten against an outside wall to tenderize it, but it is simpler to thump it with a bottle, turning it several times. Wash it again and split into individual tentacles. Drop the octopus into boiling water containing the onion and a bottle cork, and simmer until cooked (about 45 minutes); test to see if it is slightly more tender. Turn off the heat and let it sit in the water another 15 minutes.

I've eaten it spooned directly from the pot and dressed, but it is normally served as a salad at room temperature. Chop the tentacles into short lengths, combine all the remaining ingredients in a serving bowl and taste; it should be quite piquant. Toss the pieces of octopus in this dressing. Arrange a few curly tentacle tips on top, sprinkle with parsley leaves and serve warm or cold.

MEAT, POULTRY AND GAME

Succulent roasted meats are often prepared for festive occasions, and imaginative poultry and game dishes are delicious everyday fare.

CORDERO ASADO CON ALIOLI DE MEMBRILLO *(p 101)*.

No cuisine in Europe is so distinctive as Spanish meat cooking. Strong on game, poor on beef, it has a long and different tradition. The Moors left behind a liking for spices, above all cinnamon, saffron and, nowadays, paprika, which appear in many sauces along with the beloved almond. Then there is the Arab taste for sweet-and-sour, which was given new impetus with the coming of the sweet red pepper. There is also a sophisticated appreciation of fat, which is exactly balanced by acidity in a dish such as duck *a la sevillana*, where bitter orange juice and olives counteract the natural fat of the bird.

Festive cuisine, with its superb roasts and grills, is the most immediately appealing. Exquisite lamb, grazed in the mountains of central and western Spain, is the luxury meat. Milk-fed lambs and *chotos*, kids, so tiny that a leg is a portion, are Easter fare, and no one who has eaten a roast from a great bread oven, like those at Haro or Aranda de Duero, will ever forget it. Suckling pig, just three weeks old, is marketed at Christmastime. It's a specialty in places like Segovia, where the restaurateur Cándido used to carve it with the edge of a plate to demonstrate its tenderness. Spit-roasted chickens are on sale in public squares on any weekend in the south. Roast game birds, stuffed with their own giblets, may well be the Sunday dish of rural families.

In restaurants in towns you will see the middle classes eating enormous beef steaks, *solomillos* and *chuletones*, but these are not village fare. Rather diminutive lamb chops barbecued over vine prunings are the real luxury, and pork the more common choice. The *solomillo andaluz* is not beef but from a pig, and the adage for grilling is "lamb bloody and pork burnt."

La plancha is used even more than the grill: this is a griddle that lies over the charcoal in every traditional Spanish kitchen and is built-in on modern stoves. On this *chuletas de cerdo*, pork chops, are cooked, with a dusting of paprika.

Another old-fashioned cooking tool is the pot for boiling meat. "No violets come up to the perfume which a coming *olla* casts before it," said Richard Ford. Also called a *puchero* – and *escudella i carn d'olla* in Catalonia – every region has its version. A more fanciful name is *olla podrida*, literally "rotten pot," because long cooking softens the meat to the texture of overripe fruit.

If there is a national dish, then this is it. Called a *cocido* in Madrid, meats of different origin are simmered through the day – yet there is nothing of a stew or a sauce about this dish, but clean, elemental flavors. It also produces a wonderful clear broth, *caldo*, which is served as soup. This *cocido* is Jewish in origin: a pot left to simmer for the whole of the Sabbath. It was adopted after the Jews were expelled from Spain in 1492. Pork and sausages were then added, and its almost pure meat content made it an aristocratic dish. In the 18th century, chickpeas and potatoes went in too and, as a consequence, it slipped down the social scale. The pot provided more than one course and half a week's meals, for the meat from one day was cooked again on the next, in *ropa vieja*, leftovers, or literally "old clothes."

Good stews are a rural tradition, often of game birds or rabbits, which are free. *Carne de buey*, mature ox meat, and *carne de vaca*, from cows, both stew well, while *rabo de toro al Jerez*, bull's tail braised in sherry, is the most famous dish to come from the bullfight. However *toro de lidia*, meat from fighting bulls, may not be sold by ordinary butchers. *Ternera*, often translated as veal, is neither aged, hung beef, nor pink veal, but comes from steers killed between one and two years old. As ground meat, it is used for the popular *albóndigas*, meatballs, and for stuffings.

"It is not at all uncommon to meet adults among the peasants who have never tasted meat, except bacon, the *chorizo* or a wild bird," reported *A Vagabond in Spain*, 80 odd years ago. These three still play an important role in the village kitchen. The pig is killed by a *matador*, like the bull, and the *matanza*, the slaughter which traditionally happens in mid-November, supplies cheap cuts for salting and a range of different sausages to last the winter, as well as the prized, gourmet raw ham.

Other traditional cured meats are still in demand for classic dishes like the Galician *lacón con grelos*, cured pork hock with turnip tops. The pig is also a great provider of fat, which makes plain vegetables appear richer than they are.

As people have become more prosperous, dishes based on the innards of animals or fowl have not been discarded. *Callos*, stewed tripe, remains a popular *tapa*. In village restaurants things like jellied pig's feet with chickpeas or *chanfaina*, a stew of all the pig's innards, from Extremadura, are still in demand. Liver, *hígado*, in particular is served simply or included in many dishes with the meat it comes from, while kidneys in sherry are world famous.

CORDERO ASADO CON ALIOLI DE MEMBRILLO

ROAST LEG OF LAMB WITH QUINCE ALIOLI

Roast lamb is quintessentially Spanish, and a luxury there as it is here. The unusual fruit butter that accompanies this dish comes from the Pyrenees, and illustrates the Catalan capacity for combining unexpected ingredients with brilliant results. No wonder they have taken to *nouvelle cuisine* so well! The sauce can also be made with pears, and prune *alioli* is a wonderful fruit butter for roast turkey.

The leg should be small – and ideally butchered along the natural lines of the animal to take in the whole bone – otherwise shortcut, but not a frozen leg, thawed.

SERVES 6

1 leg of baby lamb, 3 – 3½ lb, at room temperature
2 garlic cloves, finely chopped
salt and freshly ground black pepper
2 tablespoons oil
1 teaspoon paprika
¼ teaspoon rosemary
¾ cup red wine

QUINCE ALIOLI

4 garlic cloves, finely chopped
½ teaspoon salt
14 oz (1 – 1½ cups) stewed quince, or quince paste
*(*dulce de membrillo *in Spanish shops,* cotognata
in Italian grocery stores)
1 tablespoon lemon juice (if using paste)
⅓ – ½ cup olive oil

Heat the oven to 450° F. Remove any obvious lumps of fat from the underside of the lamb, which should be at room temperature. Crush the garlic to a paste with ½ teaspoon of salt, adding the oil, paprika and rosemary, and rub the paste all over the lamb. Put the meat in a roasting pan into which it fits fairly tightly, putting the trimmed fat and loose shank into the corner.

Roast 15 minutes without opening the oven door. Then baste the lamb with the fat in the pan, add the wine and baste again. Turn down the oven to 350° F.

SHEEP GRAZING UNDER TREE *Grazing land is found chiefly in the mountainous areas of central and western Spain.*

Roast 40 – 50 minutes for 3 lb, 50 – 60 minutes for 4 lb, basting once.

Meanwhile, make the *alioli*. Crush the garlic and salt to a paste in a mortar or with the flat of a knife on a hard board. Be conscientious about this, to avoid small lumps. Put the drained stewed fruit into a blender with 2 tablespoons of its juice, or the quince paste with lemon juice, and reduce to a purée. Add the garlic paste and blend, then pour in the oil, a little at a time, with the blender running. Fresh fruit makes a smooth pink "mayonnaise"; quince paste is stronger and surprisingly good, despite the sugar.

Remove the lamb from the oven and let rest 10 minutes. Drain the juices from the pan and skim all fat from the top. The carver should spoon a tablespoon or so of the meat juices over each portion. Serve the *alioli* in a sauce boat. A Cabernet Sauvignon goes well: those from Raimat in Lérida and Jean León in Penedès are red wine made locally, but from foreign grapes.

CORDERO
EN AJILLO PASTOR

SHEPHERDS' AROMATIC LAMB STEW

The Romans introduced bread-thickened sauces and saffron to Spain, but the fondness for spiced food came from the Moors. This shepherds' stew, which comes from the hills above Jaén in Andalusia, has many aromatics and virtually no vegetables.

Lambs in Spain are killed when very young, and in the hills the meat and bones would be chopped up together and would include some of the more perishable meats. You can replace the heart with extra lamb if you wish.

SERVES 6

5 tablespoons olive oil
8 garlic cloves
2 lb cubed lamb, trimmed of fat and gristle
1 lamb heart, split
½ lb lamb liver, cubed
2 slices of bread, torn in pieces
15 black peppercorns
15 saffron strands, soaked in 2 tablespoons hot water
1 tablespoon white wine vinegar
1 pint dry white Spanish wine, or ¼ cup dry sherry
with 1¾ cups dry white wine
salt
2 cloves
6 thyme sprigs or ½ teaspoon dried thyme

Heat the oil in a flameproof casserole. Cut 6 of the garlic cloves in half or into thirds and fry with the cubed lamb in 2–3 batches over high heat, removing the lamb when browned. Meanwhile, wash the heart inside and cut into meaty strips, discarding fat and any flaps. Add to the casserole with the liver and fry until colored, then reserve with the cooked meat.

Fry the bread pieces in the oil remaining in the pan, with the 2 remaining garlic cloves, finely chopped. Transfer to a blender. Add the peppercorns, saffron and vinegar and blend to a paste, adding a little wine if more liquid is needed.

Pour the remaining wine into the casserole and stir over low heat to deglaze the pan and pick up all the bits. Add this liquid to the blender and combine everything at low speed.

Return the meat to the casserole, season with salt, tuck in the cloves and thyme sprigs and pour the sauce over. Cook gently, covered, on top of the stove (or in the oven at 350° F) about 45 minutes, until the lamb is tender and the sauce a little reduced. Serve with *patatas fritas*, or french fries.

In Spain the wine served with this would probably be the local red Jumilla, high in alcohol like many wines in the south, without much acidity. However, the dish is a good one and deserves a Penedès like Torres Gran Coronas, with an equal amount of body and fruit, but dry and better shaped.

CARNE CON
CASTAÑAS Y PERAS

BEEF WITH CHESTNUTS AND PEARS

This lovely beef stew for fall has a nut sauce, typical of Catalonia. Here, however, the purée of almonds is augmented by fresh chestnuts, and with pears, which have an all-important touch of cinnamon.

SERVES 4

½ lb (about 1 pint) chestnuts
6 tablespoons olive oil
2 thin slices stale bread, without crusts
1 garlic clove, finely chopped
2½ lb beef chuck or round steak, in slices
salt and freshly ground black pepper
¼ cup dry white wine
5 oz ripe tomatoes, without skin or seeds
1 tablespoon flour
6 toasted almonds (see page 88)
4 pears, stewed with cinnamon and a little sugar

Make a slit in each chestnut and drop into a saucepan. Cover with water and bring to a boil. Simmer 20 minutes. Meanwhile, heat the oil in a wide flameproof casserole. Fry the bread and the garlic and reserve them.

Cut the beef across the grain into fingers. Salt and pepper them lightly and fry in batches, tossing so that the beef colors on all sides. Do not put too many in at once (if a juice forms, remove the batch and boil the liquid away). Return all the meat and add the wine and the same quantity of water. Cover and stew gently 45 minutes, checking the liquid level occasionally.

Meanwhile prepare the sauce. Peel the chestnuts, removing the brown skin. Put 2–3 tablespoons of oil in a small pan and add the chopped tomato flesh. Let this reduce to a purée and sprinkle with flour. Grind the almonds in a spice mill or small blender with the fried bread and garlic. Stir this purée into the tomato mix. Check that the meat is cooked and its gravy well reduced. Stir in the tomato mixture and the crumbled chestnuts: the sauce should coat the meat nicely. Quarter the pears, removing the core. Add them to the casserole and heat through. An easy-to-drink local red wine is Raimat Abadia, made with half Cabernet Sauvignon grapes, though a Rioja *reserva* would go well.

TERNERA CON ALCACHOFAS A LA CORDOBESA

VEAL WITH ARTICHOKES FROM CORDOBA

The town of Montilla in Andalusia gave us the word *amontillado* for a certain style of strong, medium-dry wine, though ironically we now associate it first with sherry. The wines from the Montilla-Moriles district are fortified in Spain, like sherry, and the popular Alvear *fino*, C.B., is used for both cooking and drinking. Exported Montillas are in the sherry styles but are unfortified and, as a consequence, cheaper than sherry. "Pale dry" Montilla is excellent for cooking. It

blends beautifully with veal scallops in this dish from the neighboring town of Cordoba, though leftover roast pork is nearly as good.

SERVES 4

6 fresh globe artichokes or 16-oz canned prepared bases
2 tablespoons olive oil
2 tablespoons pork fat or butter
1 onion, finely chopped
2 garlic cloves, finely chopped
8–12 small veal scallops, about 1¼ lb
salt and freshly ground black pepper
½ cup pale dry or medium-dry Montilla wine or good sherry
½–1 cup meat or chicken stock

Prepare the artichokes. Snap off the stems (if they are stringy, that means the artichokes are tough and need an extra 5 minutes' cooking). Trim the bases flat, removing small leaves. Turn on the side and cut through the top leaves just above the choke, leaving a base about 1½-inches deep. Then trim away the side leaves with a small knife until the white base shows through. Cook the bases in boiling salted water 10 minutes. Drain upside down and cool 10 minutes.

Flip off any soft leaf stumps with your thumb, revealing the choke. Use a spoon and your thumb to remove the hairy choke, leaving a smooth cup base. Depending upon the toughness of the vegetable, this needs about 5 minutes' more cooking, which in this recipe it gets once it is added to the veal. Otherwise, braise it in a dish or in boiling water.

Heat the oil and fat or butter in a wide, shallow flameproof casserole and fry the onion until softened (20 minutes on low heat), then add the garlic. Season the scallops well, then put in half of them, well spread out, and fry over high heat until colored on both sides. Remove to a plate and fry the remaining veal. Then return all the veal to the pan and sprinkle with Montilla or sherry, boiling this away.

Add the stock – for canned artichoke bases use only half the stock. Bring to the simmering point, add the quartered artichoke bases and cook 5 minutes (or heat through if using canned bases). In Cordoba a dry Montilla would certainly be served with this dish, or Chiclana, the local sherrylike Cadiz white wine.

COCIDO MADRILEÑO

MADRID BOILED MEAT DINNER

A *cocido* is a magnificent mixture of meats, which blend and exchange flavors and make that broth which is the essence of Spanish soups. In the earlier part of this century, in most middle-class households, *cocido* was a daily ritual, except for Sundays and feast days. It was made in working-class households, too, though it was a common practice to share the ham bone, which was boiled first in one pot, then again in the next.

The recipe produces soup, a separate vegetable course, if you choose so to serve it, and a dish of meat and chickpeas, which is sometimes served as a separate course, with tomato sauce.

Exactly what goes into a *cocido* depends on what your butcher or supermarket offers. It's a waste, though, to use a roast and tender chickens. This is a dish for tough meats, full of flavor and made tender only by long cooking. First, you need some salted meat, traditionally salt pork, but corned beef is a good choice or ham on (or off) the bone. Secondly, a sausage, preferably a smoked one, and blood sausage. Thirdly, a piece of fresh meat — a stewing chicken, fresh pork sides, or possibly a piece of mature beef shank, replacing the corned beef. Finally half a meat bone and a pig's foot for a rich stock.

The green vegetables are cooked in a second pot with the sausages – which is fortunate, since most of us don't own one pot big enough for everything – so the main soup is flavored with meat, instead of cheap, all-too-familiar cabbage.

1¼ cups dried chickpeas (garbanzos)
1 – 1½ lb corned brisket of beef in 1 piece
½ lb salt pork in 1 piece, or fresh pork sides
1¼ lb ham hock, with some meat attached
1¼ – 1½ lb beef marrow bone, sawn across
½ stewing chicken, or ½ roaster as second choice
1 pig's foot, split
1 whole garlic bulb
2 bay leaves
8 black peppercorns, crushed
1 small onion, studded with 2 cloves
1½ lb head Savoy green cabbage
2 carrots, in big pieces
2 leeks, in short lengths
1 lb small new potatoes: "8 the size of eggs"
2 cooking chorizos or other smoked sausage,
like kabanos
1 morcilla or 6 – 8 oz blood sausage, cut from a ring
(skinned if this is in plastic)
salt
2 tablespoons rice

Pour boiling water over the chickpeas and let soak until needed. Put the salted meat – in this list, the corned beef, salt pork or pork sides, and ham hock – into a saucepan and cover with cold water. Bring slowly to a boil and simmer 5 minutes to remove excess salt, then drain.

The dish needs a large stockpot – at least 6 quarts. Pack in all the meat, skin side down, with the beef bone. Fit the stewing chicken and pig's foot on top. Add the garlic bulb, bay leaves and peppercorns and cover with water. Bring to the simmering point, skimming off any scum that rises. Drain the chickpeas and add, then cover and simmer on the lowest possible heat 1½ hours, checking occasionally that there is enough liquid.

If you have bought a roaster chicken, add it at this point, with the onion stuck with the cloves. No other vegetables go in this pot – otherwise it would be impossible to disentangle the chickpeas.

Start the vegetable pot. Quarter the cabbage, remove the core, and put in all the vegetables with the sausages, *morcilla* and a little salt. Bring to a boil and simmer about 25 minutes, until the potatoes are cooked.

As soon as the vegetables are cooking, strain off enough broth from the meat pot – about 5 cups – to serve as soup for the first course of the meal. Put this in a saucepan, bring back to a boil, sprinkle in the rice and cook 15 minutes, then serve.

Drain the vegetables and sausages; slice the *morcilla* and *chorizos* and arrange on a plate with the potatoes. Serve this with the meat (or as a second course). Slice all the meats; remove the marrow from the bone and slice it into the chickpeas. Arrange the meats and chickpeas on a platter, moistening with a little broth.

Drink a red Rioja with Spain's national dish. The choice depends on your meat: good corned beef, strong *chorizos* and a powerful Savoy cabbage need the

MAN WITH A GUN IN LA MANCHA *Millions of birds pass over Spain on their migration to and from Africa, and game such as partridge, pheasant, quail and rabbit are found in abundance.*

cigar-box flavors of Bodegas Bilbainas' Viña Pomal: their *reservas* are often more mature than other Riojas of their age, but not oaky. However, if the balance of your dish is toward fresh pork, chicken and mild sausages, then choose the more elegantly composed Viña Arana from La Rioja Alta. Both wines have considerable acidity, but are smooth and firm, a characteristic of wine from the Rioja Alta district.

ALPARGATAS VALENCIANAS

LITTLE MEAT ESPADRILLES IN WINE SAUCE

These pork and ham patties from Valencia are unusual and rather fun. Made in advance, they are then served in a wine and cinnamon sauce. An *alpargata* is a rope-sole – better known by its French name of *espadrille*. When fried, the patties do look very like rope-soles, because the coating of egg white fries in the characteristic ring pattern.

SERVES 4 – 6

4 slices stale bread, without crusts
¾ lb ground lean pork or veal
¼ lb ground raw or smoked ham or Canadian bacon
2 garlic cloves, finely chopped
3 tablespoons finely chopped parsley
3 extra-large eggs, separated
salt and freshly ground black pepper
olive oil for frying

CINNAMON AND WINE SAUCE
1 onion, chopped
2 tablespoons olive oil
1 garlic clove, finely chopped
2 tablespoons finely chopped parsley
1 tablespoon flour
1 cup good meat or chicken stock
1 cup oaky Spanish white wine, or a dry white wine
mixed 3:1 with pale dry Montilla
1 bay leaf
⅛ teaspoon ground cinnamon

If you are using a food processor, make the bread crumbs first, then grind together the pork or veal and ham or Canadian bacon. Add the crumbs, garlic, parsley and 3 egg yolks, keeping the whites to use later for the coating. Mix everything together, seasoning well, to make a stiff pâté.

With your hands, shape the mixture into small sausages about 2 inches long, then flatten into shoe shapes. Heat 3 – 4 tablespoons of oil and fry the patties about 3 minutes on each side. Reserve them on a tray and chill at least 1 hour.

For the sauce, soften the onion in 2 tablespoons of oil until golden, adding the garlic and parsley for the last few minutes. Tipping the pan, spoon out any visible oil, then stir in the flour and cook 1 minute. Stir in the stock, wine, bay leaf and cinnamon and simmer 5 minutes.

About 15 minutes before serving, beat the egg whites with a little salt until peaks form and coat the *alpargatas*. Fry 2 – 3 minutes on each side, until colored and heated through. Reheat the sauce in a large casserole, slip in the *alpargatas* in a single layer, and simmer gently 10 minutes. Buttered zucchini sticks make a good accompaniment.

FABADA ASTURIANA

ASTURIAN BEAN AND SAUSAGE POT

From the mountains of Asturias, one of Europe's wildest and least populated lands, *fabada* makes a warm winter lining for the ribs. A variety of local specialties go into this big bean stew. Oak-smoked fresh sausages, for example, and the popular local *lacón*. This is a smoked, cured ham hock from the front leg, plus some of the meat above, sold as a pork hock if fresh. Salt-cured pig's feet and pig's ears or tails may also be included, with the hard *longaniza* sausage. Salt pork or corned beef make a less exotic substitute for them.

A variety of meats is one key to this famous dish. As in the French *cassoulet*, fat, salt and smoked meat should each be represented. The amount of meat should roughly equal that of the beans when cooked, and so should be three times their dried weight. The real secret of the dish, however, is to impregnate the vegetables with the meat flavors, by long, slow cooking. The meats are not there, like raisins in the pudding, as a reward for eating up the beans.

Faves are big fat white beans. As they have a tendency to disintegrate with the long cooking, it's simpler to omit presoaking. Traditionally, though, the beans and salt meat are soaked together overnight (instead of blanching).

Pote asturiano is a very similar, but more souplike, dish which I like because it includes some fresh vegetables. To make this, substitute potatoes for one third of the beans and add 1 lb cabbage, cut in wedges, near the end.

SERVES 6

1¾ lb (about 4½ cups) dried large white beans such as dried lima beans

1½ lb salt pork (or corned beef)

1½ lb smoked ham hock, skin slashed

1 bay leaf

6 black peppercorns, crushed

1 teaspoon paprika

20 saffron strands, soaked in 2 tablespoons hot water (or substitute another 1 teaspoon paprika)

2 tablespoons oil (optional)

4 garlic cloves

1 lb cooking chorizos or other spicy smoked sausages, like kabanos

6 oz smoked morcilla or other blood sausage

salt and freshly ground black pepper

Use a stockpot or large flameproof casserole of a minimum size of 6 quarts. In a bowl cover the beans with plenty of boiling water. Put all the salt meat – the pork and ham hock – into a pan and cover with cold water. Bring to a boil, then drain the meat and put it into the casserole.

Drain and add the beans, bay leaf, peppercorns, paprika and saffron. Add 2½ quarts water – beans will absorb 3 times their own volume. Bring slowly to a boil, then simmer very gently on minimum heat for 2 hours – a big pot on a small burner is best, and better still with a heat diffuser. Check occasionally that the beans are still covered, but do not stir. They need very gentle cooking to prevent them from breaking up.

Remove the ham hock and salt pork to a board, to cool a little. Strip off the skin and fat, and take about 2 tablespoons of chopped fat for frying (or use oil). Put this in a skillet and render enough fat for frying. Fry the garlic lightly, then spoon it into the beans. Add the sliced sausages and blood sausage to the skillet. Fry lightly on both sides, then add the sausages and their fat to the beans in the casserole and stir in gently.

Remove all the meat from the ham hock and chop into chunks. Carve the salt pork into thick slices and then into chunks. Return the meat to the casserole; simmer for a few minutes, check the seasonings and serve. The dish is distinctly spicy, so fresh green cabbage is the ideal accompaniment, with a fruity red wine. Since most Spanish wine is blended, different styles of wine are identified with brand names. The biggest *bodega* in Rioja is Campo Viejo, and their big seller in Spain is San Ascensio *2° año sin crianza* wine, which means "two years old and not aged in wood." Another household brand of young red Rioja is Banda Azul *3° año* – Ernest Hemingway's favorite wine – from Frederick Paternina, the largest exporter.

EMPANADA DE RAXÓ

GALICIAN PORK AND SAUSAGE PIE

Pies are a feature of Galicia: fish pies baked on the shore for the returning fishermen, with scallops, or cockles and corn, or meat pies, like this one, with *chorizos* in the filling. *Raxó* is dialect for "pork loin" and this pie is the equivalent of *lasagne*, a cheap and good-tempered dish for a crowd.

SERVES 8

PORK FILLING
½ lb onions, chopped
½–⅔ cup olive oil
4 garlic cloves, finely chopped
2 lb boned loin of pork, cubed, then diced
6 oz raw or smoked ham, diced
3 cooking chorizos or other fresh spicy sausage
1 lb mixed sweet peppers, seeded and chopped
1 cup canned tomatoes, with juice
¼ cup dry white wine
10 saffron strands, soaked in 2 tablespoons hot water
1 teaspoon paprika
2 tablespoons chopped parsley
salt and freshly ground black pepper
2 hard-cooked eggs, chopped

WINE PASTRY
6 tablespoons lard or margarine
2¾ cups flour, plus extra for sprinkling
1 teaspoon salt
6 tablespoons olive oil
¼ cup dry white wine
3 medium eggs, 1 of them beaten for glazing

Make the filling in advance. Fry the onions in ½ cup oil over medium heat, adding the garlic when they begin to color. Add the pork and ham and fry until colored, stirring regularly. Add 2 more tablespoons of oil if necessary, and add the chopped *chorizo* and sweet peppers. Fry gently.

Add the tomatoes, wine, saffron, paprika and parsley and season generously. Cook gently 20 minutes until the pork is done and the liquid has evaporated and thickened. Let cool.

Make the wine pastry. Use a food processor to work the fat into the flour-plus-salt, then the oil, wine and 2 eggs. Alternatively, make a well in the middle of the flour, melt the fat and pour it into the middle, then work everything in gradually with your fingers. Blend to a smooth pastry and chill 15–20 minutes.

Heat the oven with a baking sheet to 375° F. Choose a small roasting pan or large rectangular ovenproof dish, between 12 × 8 inches and 11 inches square. This is a handy pie, as there is no problem if the container is too big, because of the way the pastry folds.

Divide the pastry in half, then pull off a piece (small egg size) and add it to the base pastry. Roll out the bottom layer thinly, so it is large enough just to hang over the container sides. Lift it, rolled around the rolling pin, and press gently into the container. Smooth the cold filling into the pastry case and sprinkle with the chopped egg.

Trim off overhanging pastry, to just below the rim on the outside of the container, then fold it inward over the meat and brush the turnover with egg. Roll out the lid and place on top. Press the two together all around with a fork: this is characteristic of the pie. Brush with more egg and prick the surface. Bake on the hot sheet 40 minutes. Cabbage goes well with the pie, freshly boiled, or part-cooked then fried with garlic, and, to accompany it, any expansive fruity red wine. Ribera del Duero comes from northern Spain, but there is a wide choice of regional Spanish wine, simply labeled *reserva*.

EMPANADA DE RAXÓ *top,* POLLO EN CHILINDRÓN *bottom (p 110).*

POLLO EN CHILINDRÓN

CHICKEN WITH SWEET RED PEPPER, HAM AND TOMATOES

Aragon is sometimes described as the "zone of *chilindrónes*," so popular is this dish, which is also made with lamb and pork. In *Viaje por La Cocina Española*, Luis Antonio de Vega describes a custom, dating back to Moorish times, for workmen joining a workshop to treat their mates to this dish. Later on it was eaten to seal a bargain – and referred to as "the tip."

SERVES 4

3¼-lb chicken, quartered and backbone removed
salt and freshly ground black pepper
2 teaspoons paprika
2 tablespoons olive oil
1 onion, chopped
½ lb smoked or raw ham, diced
3 sweet red peppers, chopped
2 garlic cloves, finely chopped
½ cup drained canned tomatoes
½ small dried chili pepper, seeded and chopped

Remove the wing tips and rub salt and paprika into the chicken portions. Heat the oil in a flameproof casserole into which the chicken will fit comfortably and put in the chicken portions, skin side down. Fry over medium-low heat, turning until golden on all sides.

While the chicken is cooking, distribute the onion and diced ham in the gaps in the casserole and fry, stirring every now and then, until soft. Chicken gives off its fat, so you may be able to remove a couple of spoonfuls of oil at this point.

Pour boiling water over the chopped sweet pepper and let soak 10 minutes. Drain well, then blot on paper towels. If you have a food processor, pulse briefly (this is not crucial, however).

If the pan is very full, you may find it easier to take out the chicken briefly. Add the garlic, sweet peppers and chopped tomato to the pan, with the dried chili pepper. Cook and let it reduce 4–5 minutes, check salt and pepper, then cook covered (with the chicken) 10 minutes. Small new potatoes go well with this.

Quintessentially Spanish, and no worse for being a working-class dish, this chicken calls for a red wine that is unmistakably from the same country, with a hint of the oak cask about it – a characteristic all Riojas share. *Reservas* are a minimum of four years old, with one year at least in the barrel (and often more), well-balanced wines, with a satisfying long aftertaste. Try a Viña Herminia Lagunilla *reserva*, 2 years in the barrel, or the fresh, lighter Viña Albina *reserva*.

STREET IN MADRID *A solitary lamppost casts its shadow in the baking heat of the midday sun.*

MEADOW IN EXTREMADURA (overleaf) *A carpet of purple clover puts on a dazzling display.*

PEPITORIA DE GALLINA

CHICKEN FRICASSEE WITH ALMOND SAUCE

A *pepita* is a tiny seed – pine nuts, sunflower seeds, even melon seeds and tomato seeds are all covered by the word – though almonds are now used in this dish rather than the original pine nuts. The dish is Moorish and dates back at least to the 13th century. A *gallina* is a hen, and I guess it was a tough one, for the old recipe stewed it for a long time in stock, which was then thickened with hard-cooked egg yolks as well as the almonds which are used in the modern recipe.

SERVES 4

25 blanched almonds
about ¼ cup olive oil
2 garlic cloves, finely chopped
1 thick slice bread, without crusts
3-lb chicken, cut up (see page 22), without wing tips
salt and freshly ground black pepper
5 saffron strands
½ cup good chicken stock
½ cup pale dry Montilla wine or fino *sherry*
1 bay leaf, crumbled
4 sprigs of fresh thyme
1 tablespoon parsley, chopped so finely "it becomes invisible"
tiny pinch of freshly grated nutmeg
tiny pinch of powdered clove
1 teaspoon lemon juice

Start the sauce. Toast the almonds in a low oven (about 300° F) shaking the pan occasionally, until they are very lightly browned and give off a pleasant smell.

Heat the oil in a wide, shallow flameproof casserole, frying the garlic and removing it before the oil gets too hot. Over high heat, fry the bread quickly on both sides, then reserve it with the garlic.

Season the chicken pieces well and fry them in the casserole, turning till golden on all sides – about 20 minutes.

Remove the chicken from the pot and drain off any excess oil. Dissolve the saffron in a cup with 2 tablespoons of hot stock, then add the remaining stock, with the Montilla, to the pot, stirring to deglaze the bottom. Return the chicken to the pot, add the bay leaf and thyme and cover. Cook gently 10 minutes.

Make the sauce: grind the toasted almonds in a small blender, then add the bread in pieces, the garlic, parsley, saffron liquid, nutmeg and clove and reduce to an aromatic purée. Stir this into the chicken juices, with the lemon juice, and serve. Snow peas make a fresh accompaniment.

PERDIZ EN CHOCOLATE

PARTRIDGE WITH CHOCOLATE SAUCE

Partridge is almost an everyday dish in many rural families, by far and away the most popular of game birds in Spain. The red-legged (or French) partridge is native to southwest Europe and, once trapped, the birds are often kept in cages hanging outside the house. Four squab can be substituted, but in this case use about ⅔ cup extra stock.

Chocolate is quite common in game sauces all over Spain, particularly with rabbit. It gives the sauce a deliciously subtle flavor for, of course, it is not naturally sweet. This dish comes from Valladolid in Castile, but similar dishes are cooked all along the Pyrenees. In Catalonia, chocolate sauce is even served with lobster.

SERVES 4

2 partridge, cleaned
2 tablespoons Spanish brandy
salt and freshly ground black pepper
3 tablespoons pork fat or olive oil
1 onion, chopped
3 garlic cloves, finely chopped
about 2 tablespoons flour
1 cup red wine
1 cup good chicken stock
¼ cup wine vinegar
6 black peppercorns
2 cloves
1 bay leaf
8 shallots or pearl onions
3 carrots, in short lengths
1 oz unsweetened chocolate, grated

Reach into the neck of each bird, run finger and thumb nails up the wishbone to the top and pull it out. Halve the birds, cutting on both sides of the backbone and on one side of the breastbone. Blot inside with paper towels. Rub the birds with brandy, salt and pepper, then let them sit 30 minutes.

Heat the fat or oil in a flameproof casserole into which the birds will fit snugly, and fry the onion gently, adding the garlic as it softens. Sprinkle the birds lightly with flour and fry about 5 minutes each

side until colored.

Pour in the wine and stock and add the vinegar, peppercorns, cloves and bay leaf. Bring to the simmering point, then cover and cook very gently 40 minutes. Add the pearl onions, if using, then 5 minutes later the carrots; shallots should go in with the carrots. Simmer another 15 minutes.

Spoon the birds and vegetables from the pan. Reduce the sauce by boiling if there is more than about $1\frac{1}{4} - 1\frac{1}{2}$ cups, then purée in a blender. Return to the pan and add the chocolate, stirring until it is melted. Arrange the partridge and vegetables back in the casserole, spooning a little sauce over them. Serve with a good Rioja *reserva*.

PERDIZ EN CHOCOLATE

PATO CON HIGOS

ROAST DUCK WITH DRIED FIGS

Ducks and figs have been linked for centuries – the birds love to feed on the half-ripe fruit that never matures. The Romans were the first to discover the beneficial effect that figs had on the duck's liver. It seems appropriate, therefore, to make this Pyrenean dish with a gray Barbary duck, the type traditionally used for fattening livers for *foie gras*. These birds have started appearing in supermarkets and have gamy meat and far less fat than white ducks.

Dried figs have a beautiful affinity with *amontillado*

sherry, and the sauce is just lifted from sweetness by the lemon oil in the fresh zest, added at the last moment. Bunches of dressed watercress will add color.

SERVES 4

4-lb duckling, or 3½-lb Barbary duck
salt and freshly ground black pepper
2 tablespoons pork fat or butter
1 onion, finely chopped
2 garlic cloves, finely chopped
1 cup giblet or chicken stock
10 oz (about 2 cups) ready-to-eat dried figs
1 cup amontillado or dry oloroso sherry
grated zest of ½ lemon

116

Heat the oven; if using a white duck, to 400° F; if using a Barbary duck, to 425° F. Prick the duck fat all over and season the bird inside and out. Melt the pork fat or butter in a roasting pan into which the duck just fits and put it in, breast side down. Cook on top of the stove, turning it over and propping it against the edge, until colored on all sides. Drain and reserve the fat and put the duck in the oven to roast – about 1¼ hours for a duck at the lower temperature, 35–40 minutes for a Barbary duck.

Meanwhile, use 2 tablespoons of the duck fat to sweat the onion in a saucepan until soft, adding the garlic toward the end. Add the stock and let it reduce and concentrate. In another pan simmer the figs in the sherry 10 minutes. Then drain as much fat as you can from the roasting pan and baste the duck with ½ cup of the fig juice.

Reserve 8 figs for a garnish and purée the remaining figs and juice with the stock and onion in a blender. Return to the pan.

Remove the duck to a warm serving platter to rest. Strain off the fat from the roasting pan and add the juices to the sauce. Add the lemon zest and check the seasoning. Quarter the duck and serve garnished with figs and accompanied by the sauce. With it serve a red wine from the Rioja Alta, such as a Viña Ardanza *reserva*, an unmistakably Spanish wine with an immediate oaky aroma and often a rich, creamy vanilla taste, that it is almost like a dessert.

CODORNICES ASADAS CON AJOS

ROAST QUAIL WITH GARLIC CLOVES

Quail are wild birds in Spain, trapped by nets as they fly through the mountain passes during migration twice a year. You might find this simple country dish in any small *venta* or roadside eatery, usually served with

FLOCK OF SHEEP IN ZAMORA *The exquisite roast lamb of Castile is highly regarded throughout Spain.*

mounds of french fries, though *patatas picantes* (see page 71) are good too.

Other small birds can be roasted the same way: for 2 partridge allow 30–35 minutes, or roast a single guinea fowl 40–45 minutes, turning it 3 times.

SERVES 4

8 small quail
24 garlic cloves
salt and freshly ground black pepper
6 tablespoons olive oil
flour
¼ cup red wine or sweet Malaga wine

To prepare the quail, snip off the wings at the joint, if they are still there, then reach into the quail's neck and find the wishbone on each side with your thumb and index finger. Run the nails up to the top of the wishbone and pinch it out. It is then possible to eat the cooked birds neatly with a knife and fork.

Cut across the stem end of the garlic cloves with a big kitchen knife, then lay the flat of the knife on them in turn and press. This pops off the skin and crushes them. Put a small clove into each quail, and salt and pepper the birds.

Heat the oven to 425° F with a roasting pan containing the oil and the remaining crushed garlic cloves. Put in the birds breast side down (this saves all the business of barding them with bacon) and roast 10 minutes. Turn them over, basting them well, and shake the merest dusting of flour through a sifter onto the breasts. Add the wine to the pan and cook another 10–15 minutes, when they will be crispy on top.

Move the birds to a serving platter, garnishing them with the garlic cloves, which are now quite mild, and spoon off all the oil from the pan. Serve 2 quail per person, with a spoonful of pan juices.

Our farmed quail taste less of game than wild birds, so try a light but balanced fruity red Senoria de Los Llanos *Gran Reserva* from Valdepeñas. With partridge or guinea fowl, however, a bottle of Torres Sangredetoro, which is full-bodied and fruity, would show to advantage. It is one of the few Penedès wines made from native grapes and still typical of wine produced in the region in times past.

ESCABECHE DE PERDICES

SOUSED PARTRIDGE

The Arabs invented pickling in vinegar as a means of keeping cooked meat fresh – the word *escabeche* comes from the Persian *sikbāj*, "acid food." In Spain, however, the method was enthusiastically adopted for fish. It then traveled inland, and has become a specialty for game birds and rabbit in Old Castile.

A convenient party food, I was once served this old-fashioned dish with a *nouvelle cuisine* garnish, which suited it well.

SERVES 4

2 partridge, cleaned
salt and freshly ground black pepper
2 tablespoons olive oil
1 small onion, chopped
1 celery stalk, diced small
4 garlic cloves, finely chopped
¾ cup dry white wine
¾ cup tarragon vinegar
¾ cup chicken stock
2 cloves
1 bay leaf
2 sprigs fresh thyme or a pinch of dried thyme
4 carrots
½ head lettuce

Reach into the neck of each bird and run finger and thumb nails up the wishbone to the top and pull it out. Salt and pepper the birds. Choose a pot into which they fit snugly side by side. Heat the oil in the pot and fry the birds, turning them over and propping them against the sides of the pot, until they are colored on all sides. Remove the birds.

Fry the onion in the same pot until soft, adding the chopped celery and then the garlic when the onion starts to soften. Pull the vegetables to the sides of the pot and put in the birds, packing the pot tightly. Add the wine, vinegar, stock, cloves, bay leaf and thyme, and bring gently to a boil. Simmer 1 hour, adding water to keep the birds covered. Transfer the partridge to a 6-inch diameter dish (without using your fingers). They should be packed in tightly and completely covered with the stock, when this is poured in.

The stock will jell around the birds, which will keep for a week.

To serve, split the birds in 2, cutting out the backbones. Arrange in a dish with a little jellied stock (melting it and glazing the birds, if you wish). Make the garnish. For carrot "flowers," make grooves lengthwise down the carrot on all sides with a canelle cutter or fork, then cut in rounds and cook briefly. Roll some lettuce leaves in wads, then cut across to make ribbons. Arrange around the birds.

A Navarra red would go well with the cold birds. This district adjoins Rioja and shares many of its wine characteristics. What these wines lack in finesse they make up for in fresh fruitiness – needed here to balance the vinegar.

CONEJO GUISADO A LA BURGALESA

STEWED RABBIT FROM BURGOS

Most regions of Spain have their own recipes for rabbit: with garlic in La Mancha, with rosemary in Catalonia. Rabbit are frequently cooked with another free food – snails – which feed on rosemary and therefore act as a walking *bouquet garni*. Serve this stew from the heart of Old Castile with boiled carrots or fried mushrooms with thyme.

SERVES 6

5-lb rabbit (or 2 small ones), giving 3 lb meat, in
6 serving portions
salt and freshly ground black pepper
2 oz pork fat or ¼ cup olive oil
1 rabbit liver (or turkey liver)
2 onions, chopped
1 celery stalk, chopped
4 garlic cloves, finely chopped
¾ cup white wine
1¼ cups chicken stock
2 ripe tomatoes, without skin or seeds, chopped
1 bay leaf
1 sprig thyme
grating of fresh nutmeg
chopped parsley for garnish

With 4 legs and the saddle split lengthwise, a rabbit makes 6 portions. Season the meat and heat the fat or oil in a shallow flameproof casserole in which the rabbit will fit in one layer. Fry the hind legs 5 minutes, turning, then add the remaining portions and cook until golden on all sides. Remove the meat, then fry the liver 2 minutes on each side and reserve it. Add the onion to the pan with the celery and cook until softened, adding the garlic toward the end. Return the rabbit to the pan and add the wine, stock, crushed tomato, bay leaf and thyme. Grate a tiny amount of nutmeg over the top. Simmer, covered, 45 minutes or until tender.

Remove the rabbit to a serving dish. Purée the liver in a blender and stir into the sauce to thicken it. Check the seasonings, including the nutmeg, then spoon over the rabbit. Sprinkle with a little parsley. Rabbit never divides into fair portions – the hind legs have most meat and the saddle is good for those who hate bones.

VENADO ASADO CON SALSA DE CABRALES

ROAST VENISON WITH BLUE CHEESE SAUCE

There are still bears and wolves in the mountains of the Picos de Europa in northern Spain, one of the largest wild areas in Europe. Chamois and deer run here in considerable numbers.

The region also produces Spain's most delicious cheese, Cabrales. Moist and blue, matured in caves with stalactites and sent to market wrapped in plane leaves, it is similar to Roquefort. I have eaten this same sauce made with Roquefort, in a different range of Spanish mountains, the Pyrenees, where Roquefort is a local ingredient. On that occasion it was served with boned, rolled, roast pork loin.

SERVES 6

1½-lb boned venison loin, or 2½-lb boned haunch or leg, sold rolled, tied and barded with pork fat
1 pint red wine (for leg)
salt and freshly ground black pepper
3–4 tablespoons butter or pork fat

BLUE CHEESE SAUCE
2 tablespoons Fundador or another Spanish brandy
1 cup whipping cream
3 oz Cabrales or Roquefort cheese

A loin of venison roasts like a beef tenderloin – it is more expensive, but wonderfully tender and less meat is needed, because the long thin shape makes neat slices. A roast from the top of the leg is more like beef top round – a wider cut, slightly coarser and more likely to shrink in the oven; more is needed. The leg is often sold with a covering of pork fat, to prevent it drying out during roasting. It is also tougher and so it is wise to marinate it beforehand. Remove the barding and string, put the leg in a small but deep bowl, pour the wine over and leave 24 hours, turning once.

Heat the oven to 400° F. Season the venison. Melt the butter or fat in a small roasting pan, put in the venison and turn it to seal all sides. Move to the oven and roast a loin 25 minutes and a leg roll (retied, with the barding fat back in place) 50 minutes, basting the meat at least once. Let the roast rest on a warm serving platter.

Spoon off the fat from the roasting pan, if the meat was barded. Put it over low heat and add the brandy, stirring to pick up the juices. Add the cream and boil to reduce a little. Mash in the crumbled cheese with a spoon. Carve a loin into 6 uniform slices and serve on a platter. Carve the rolled leg at the table, and serve the sauce in a sauceboat.

With this, drink a local wine, like Vega de Toro *tinto reserva*. Full-bodied, deep in color with something of black currant about it, this wine comes from the newest of Spain's *appellation contrôlée* districts, although Toro is reputedly the oldest red wine in Spain. It went with Columbus to America and has been called the "thinking wine," because it has been patronized by the University of Salamanca since the 13th century.

MORTERUELO

HARE, CHICKEN, HAM AND LIVER TERRINE

Don Quixote ate this peasant dish at El Toboso in La Mancha, nearly 400 years ago. It's a typical mixture of game and the cheaper meats from the farm: *gazpacho manchego* has the same mixture. Only the bony front part of the hare is included, reserving the prime meat of the saddle and back legs for roasting.

The classic method is to pulverize everything together in a mortar – which gives the hash its name – and serve it hot. But with three such different meats I prefer to shred them and serve the dish cold as unusually seasoned, coarse-textured pâté.

SERVES 12 – 15

14 oz smoked ham
2 hare front legs and rib cage, about 1¼ lb
½ chicken, about 1½ lb including backbone
1 pig's foot, split
3 cups dry white wine
1 lb pork fat back, cubed
2 onions, finely chopped
6 garlic cloves, finely chopped
1¼ lb lamb liver, trimmed and cubed
2 teaspoons salt
freshly ground black pepper
2 teaspoons paprika
¼ teaspoon ground cinnamon
½ teaspoon ground cumin
⅛ teaspoon ground clove
6 tablespoons chopped parsley
1½ cups fresh bread crumbs
½ cup coarsely chopped walnuts

Put the ham in a saucepan, cover with cold water and bring to a boil. Simmer 5 minutes, then drain. Split the hare legs from the rib cage and pack the hare, chicken, ham and pig's foot into a pot. Cover with the wine and simmer 40 minutes.

SHUTTERED HOUSE *With its lowered shutters and sleepy air, the house, as well as its inhabitants, seems to be enjoying a* siesta.

Chop the pork fat and heat in a skillet until it renders its fat; pour into a heatproof measuring cup until there is 1 cup. Discard the bits from the pan, then use some fat from the measuring cup to fry the onion gently until softened, adding the garlic toward the end. Turn the onion into a food processor, or better still a blender.

When the chicken will come easily off the bone, remove it to a well-scrubbed board and pick all the meat off it with two forks (no fingers should be used from now on as the dish is to be kept). Pick the meat into shreds and transfer to a shallow serving bowl, about 2½-quart capacity. Return the bones and skin to the pot and continue simmering. Transfer the ham to the board and remove the rind and fat. Break up the meat into shreds and add to the chicken in the bowl.

Heat more fat in the skillet and fry the liver in 3 batches over high heat, sprinkling it with salt and plenty of freshly ground pepper. Add the liver to the onions in the blender when cooked. Reduce them to a purée, adding the paprika, cinnamon, cumin and clove. Heat all but about 3 tablespoons of the remaining fat in the skillet, return the liver purée to the heat and fry it gently.

Pick the hare meat off the bones and add to the bowl. Discard the pig's foot, strain the juices from the pot and add to the liver. Then stir in the parsley with the bread crumbs and walnuts to stiffen the hash. Finally add all the shredded meat and check the seasoning. Traditionally this is served hot. To serve cold, pack into the serving bowl, smoothing the top with the back of a spoon. Warm the remaining fat and spoon it over the top, chill and let mature 48 hours. Serve with French bread.

DESSERTS AND
DRINKS

*Spain is blessed with a mouthwatering
abundance of fresh fruit and a
dessert-making tradition of depth and
subtlety, in which Moorish influences are
unmistakable.*

FRESAS CON ANIS *left (p 138)*, MANTECADOS *right (p 134)*.

THE GRAPES WERE "as big as plums, the melons melted on the tongue like snow, the wine was fiery and potent," raved Hans Christian Andersen, visiting Valencia in the 1860s. With apples in the Pyrenees, peach orchards in Navarre, melons in Lérida, pomegranates named after Granada, plums drying for Christmas alongside the chilies in Rioja and muscatel grapes on the hot coasts of Valencia and Alicante, Spain claims the best fruit in the world, and, appropriately, fruit ends most Spanish meals.

Oranges are almost the symbol of Spain, introduced by the Moors a couple of centuries before the Crusaders took them to Sicily and Italy. Our so-called "Sevilles" were planted in the beautiful courtyards of the Alhambra in Granada and throughout the south. With them came lemons and the forerunner of the grapefruit. Sweet oranges came in the 15th century.

At almost all other times of the day, apart from *postre*, "afters," the Spanish sweet tooth is gratified by a range of dessert wines and liqueurs and special-occasion candies, some of almost Oriental sugariness. Almonds and honey are included in many of them. *Turrón*, or nougat, white or dark, soft or brittle, is exceedingly more-ish and is now a big industry in Jijona. The Arabic influences in candy-making are pronounced and candies such as *amarguillos* date from Moorish times.

They might shy away from the idea, but the nuns of innumerable orders are the direct successors to the Moors, as candy-makers. The reason is that egg whites are used to clarify sherry and even red wine, and the yolks have then traditionally been given away for charity. From them the nuns created specialties to sell, sometimes their only source of income. *Yemas*, meaning "yolks," are combined with sugar and the names of the candies come from their shape, like *rosquillas*, rings, or from the order which cherishes the recipe, like San Leandro in Seville or Santa Teresa in Avila.

In the Spanish kitchen, milk and cream are commandeered for desserts, particularly in the north. Curds and junket, *cuajardan*, are served with spoonfuls of honey and cold rice milk pudding, *arroz con leche*, is popular. Much richer sweets are made from custard, often fried in squares as *leche frita*. Chilled *natilla*, a custard deeply flavored with cinnamon and lemon zest, is found all over Spain. The national dessert, however, is caramel custard, called *flan*. A blissful southern version, made with syrup rather than milk, is called *tocino de cielo* – "heavenly bacon," which is exactly how it looks.

Ices have a 1,000-year history in Spain, for even the south has high mountains, and in the 19th century Washington Irving noted the snow-gatherers working at night in the Sierra Nevada, to rush ice to Granada before dawn. The favorite ice creams are delicious lemon sorbets packed into their own shells and cinnamon ice cream, which is preferred to vanilla.

The Spanish discoveries in the Americas changed Spanish desserts by making sugar cheap, and establishing "burnt" sugar as a very Spanish taste. With sugar came chocolate, used originally for drinks but not sweets, and a Spanish monopoly for over a century. More important, the association of chocolate with cinnamon began and this persists in Spain, though vanilla has long since taken over elsewhere. Curiously, the *conquistadores* missed the vanilla bean entirely.

Rich, sweet little cookies hold pride of place in the festival kitchen. All over Spain you may find *polvorones*, *mantecados y almendrados* – crumble cakes, lardy cakes or almond cookies – which are ideal companions to wine. Pine nuts go into *piñonates* and *mostachónes*, S-shaped biscuits which make "mustaches" in pairs.

Little choux puffs like *buñuelos* are made for Saints' days, particularly for that of San Isidro, the patron saint of Madrid, and deep-fried and stuffed *huesos de santo*, saint's bones, are made for All Saints on November 1st, though these are becoming harder to find. The marzipan *figuritas* of Toledo are eaten everywhere at Christmas. Spaniards are also fond of sweet pastries, like the ground almond *tarta de Santiago*, found on many tables on St James' day, topped with a stencil of St James' big sword in powdered sugar.

From Moorish times drinks were offered with sweets as a gesture of hospitality. Spanish brandy is perfumed and sweet and there is a fondness for sweet alcohols like anise. The day may start with a sweet, thick chocolate drink, while *horchata*, a milk made from tiger nuts and sometimes iced, suits the morning or late afternoon. Hot weather brings *leche merengada*, chilled milk with meringue, on to café menus. There are also long drinks of wines with citrus juice, like *sangría*, and the less-known Basque punch, *linoyada*, with red and white wines. And for the night, there are regional punches, like *queimada*, which can blow your legs away.

CREMA CATALANA

BURNT CATALAN CREAM

The Catalans claim to have invented caramelized sugar, and this classic custard, with its Middle Eastern flavors of cinnamon and lemon, justifies the name of "burnt cream" far better than *crème brûlée*. The caramel forms the merest net on top and it tastes delicately caramelized rather than of toffee. The sugar is traditionally caramelized with a salamander, a round branding iron, about 2 inches across, on a long handle, which is heated to red-hot. These are sometimes sold in gourmet and kitchenware stores.

The easiest and neatest way of all to caramelize sugar, however, is with a small blowtorch (of the type used for paint-stripping). This way a fine layer of brittle caramel is possible. Domestic broilers rarely get hot enough to melt the sugar quickly, so a thick, impervious layer is needed to protect the custard.

SERVES 6

1 cup milk
1 cup light cream
4 strips of lemon zest
1 cinnamon stick
4 extra-large egg yolks
1 tablespoon cornstarch
½ cup granulated sugar
¼ cup raw brown sugar for topping

Heat the milk and cream with the lemon zest and cinnamon stick to the simmering point, then leave, off the heat, to infuse 20 minutes. Beat together the egg yolks, cornstarch and granulated sugar with a wooden spoon until light and fluffy.

Remove the cinnamon and lemon zest from the milk, bring gently back to a simmer and pour onto the yolks. Return the mixture to the saucepan and stir gently over low heat. Mercifully this custard doesn't need a double-boiler, because the cornstarch avoids any risk of curdling. When the custard will coat the spoon, pour it into 6½-cup-capacity earthenware dishes or ramekins and chill.

About 30 minutes before serving, sprinkle brown sugar lightly over the top of each custard and then give them 15–20 seconds of intense heat – a low blast from the blowtorch. (The caramel melts in the custard, if done too far ahead.) You can try caramelizing these under the hottest part of your broiler, but I can't promise this will be successful. They are also good plain and served very cold. Return to the refrigerator until ready to serve. The cream is luscious with a chilled glass of Bach Extrésimo *blanco semi dulce*. This is not a Muscat wine and is surprisingly refreshing for a sweet Spanish white, with a drop of honey in the finish.

MARQUESA DE CHOCOLATE VALENCIANA

VALENCIA CHOCOLATE MOUSSE

Unusually for a Spanish dessert, this chocolate mousse is not very sweet. Yet it is the lightest, most chocolatey dessert in the world.

SERVES 6

4 oz best quality semisweet chocolate, broken into small pieces
3 tablespoons cocoa powder (unsweetened)
4 tablespoons unsalted butter, diced
2 extra-large egg yolks
3 extra-large egg whites
2 tablespoons superfine sugar
chopped crystallized orange peel for decoration

Melt the chocolate carefully in a bowl over barely simmering water, stirring and making sure the bottom doesn't cook. Stir in the cocoa powder. Remove from the heat and beat in the butter until smooth.

Stir the egg yolks into the chocolate mixture. Beat the egg whites to soft peaks. Sprinkle the sugar over the whites and beat 2–3 minutes to make a glossy meringue. Spoon the chocolate over the top in 2–3 batches and fold in with a big spoon, cutting it down into the meringue with the spoon edge.

Spoon into 6 small ramekins, ⅓-cup capacity, or small straight-sided wineglasses. Decorate the tops with a little chopped crystallized orange peel and chill until needed. Málaga *dulce*, the golden Mountain wine, goes perfectly with it.

FLAN DE NARANJA

ORANGE CARAMEL CREAMS

If Spain has a national dessert, it is *flan*: a delicate little castle of custard, topped with melted caramel, and nothing to do with pastry. This Valencian version is made with orange juice rather than milk, a few sweet spoonfuls only, and with its beautiful texture is perfect to end a meal.

SERVES 6

1¼ cups granulated sugar
2–3 large oranges, ⅞ cup juice
7 extra-large egg yolks
1 extra-large egg

Heat the oven to 325° F and arrange 6 ramekins, ⅓-cup capacity, or *demi-tasse* coffee cups (not valuable ones), in a small roasting pan.

Put ¼ cup sugar in a small pan with 2 tablespoons of water for the caramel and heat gently, stirring to dissolve the sugar. Let it boil until it turns light brown and smells of caramel, then remove it immediately from the heat. Quickly pour about 1 tablespoonful into the bottom of each ramekin or cup, turning it to coat the bottom and a little of the sides.

Grate the zest from 1 orange on your finest grater, then use a little of the remaining sugar to mop up the shreds and the orange oil from the grater. Put the yolks and whole egg in a bowl and beat lightly with a wooden spoon to combine them. Bring the orange juice and sugar to the boiling point, stirring to dissolve the sugar, then turn down the heat and boil for 2 minutes.

Pour the hot juice onto the yolks, stirring, then strain. Divide the mixture between the ramekins in the pan (they won't be quite full). Pour boiling water around them, to come two thirds of the way up the sides of the ramekins. Bake 30 minutes, remove the pan from the oven and leave the ramekins in the water until cool enough to handle, then chill. Serve the creams unmolded, with a little of their caramel syrup spooned around them.

TARTA QUEMADA HELADA

ORANGE ICE CREAM WITH BRITTLE CARAMEL

The Spaniards are extremely fond of ice creams, which are sold everywhere but less often made at home. This combination of luscious orange-studded ice cream and crisp caramel is absolutely stunning.

A *tarta* simply means a "dessert" and, like so many others in Andalusia, this one contains numerous egg yolks as these are a by-product of sherry-making.

SERVES 8

¼ cup chopped crystallized orange peel
1 tablespoon Grand Marnier or Triple Sec (optional)
8 extra-large egg yolks
½ cup granulated sugar
1¼ cups milk, hot
1 teaspoon vanilla extract
1¼ cups whipping cream
about 1½ cups raw brown sugar

Soak the peel in the orange liqueur if it seems hard. Beat the yolks and granulated sugar until creamy in a bowl which fits over a pan of simmering water. Pour the hot milk onto the yolks, add the vanilla and stir until the custard is thick – the bowl must not touch the water. Press a piece of plastic wrap down on the surface of the custard to prevent a skin forming, and leave until cold.

Whip the cream until thick, then fold in the orange peel and liqueur. Fold the cream into the custard. Spoon into 8 ramekins or small shallow baking dishes, no more than three quarters full, and chill, then freeze until firm.

Heat the broiler until very hot. Spread about 2 tablespoons of brown sugar over the top of each dish and broil under the hottest spot, in batches if necessary, until caramelized – up to 2 minutes. Remove the ramekins to cool in a sink in a little cold water, then chill and return to the freezer for about 3 hours.

Allow the *tartas* 30 minutes out of the freezer in the refrigerator before serving, to soften slightly. The caramel top will be brittle and the ice cream is so rich it should be eaten slowly, ideally with a glass of Freixenet, the popular Spanish *champán*.

TARTA AL WHISKY

FROZEN WHISKEY LAYER CAKE

From Galicia in the north across the country to the Mediterranean in the south, most restaurants offer this ice cream cake. It is made by all the big ice cream manufacturers and is favored for Sunday lunch out, which in Spain is a family affair. It can be delicious or indifferent – like Black Forest cake in southern Germany which suffers the same fate. Homemade, it is genuinely good. It's a clever ice too, because it has two layers of different vanilla ice creams, one incorporating the egg yolks, the other made with the egg whites.

SERVES 12

sponge-cake recipe (see page 133)
¼ cup whiskey

GOLDEN VANILLA ICE CREAM
6 extra-large egg yolks
½ cup granulated sugar
2 cups milk
1 teaspoon vanilla extract
¼ cup whiskey
¼ cup praline (see recipe below)
1 cup whipping cream

WHITE VANILLA ICE CREAM
4 egg whites
¼ cup superfine sugar
1 cup whipping cream
1 teaspoon vanilla extract

PRALINE, CARAMEL AND DECORATION
1¼ cups granulated sugar
1 cup shelled almonds
½ cup shelled hazelnuts
½ cup whipping cream

Make the cake batter and bake it in a 9½-inch springform cake pan at 350° F for 15 minutes. Cool on a wire rack.

Make the praline. Heat ½ cup sugar with 2 tablespoons of water in a saucepan until caramelized to a light brown. Add the nuts, stir 1 minute, then pour onto a piece of greased tin foil. When cold (quite soon), break up the sheet of nuts and caramel, and chop coarsely. Chop a generous ¼ cup more finely, and reserve this for flavoring the golden ice cream.

Use the same pan to make the caramel for the top of the cake. Cover a flat baking sheet with foil and draw around the cake pan with a ballpoint pen. Make the caramel, and pour into the circle. Spread with the back of the spoon, keeping just inside the line. Immediately mark the disk across with a long knife dipped in hot water, to make 12 portions.

Make the golden vanilla ice cream. Prepare a double-boiler with a little simmering water in the bottom. Cream the egg yolks in the top pan (off the heat) with 2 tablespoons of sugar. Heat half the milk with the remaining sugar and the vanilla until boiling. Pour onto the yolks, stirring all the time. Put the pan over the hot water and stir gently until the custard will coat the spoon (about 15 minutes). Add the remaining milk and leave until cold, stirring occasionally.

Add the whiskey and finely chopped praline and fold in the whipped cream. Freeze in an ice cream maker, or in the freezer, beating after 2 hours. Smooth the ice cream into the same pan that was used for baking the cake and freeze for 2 hours.

Cut the cake into 3 layers (freeze the other layers to use on another occasion). Cover the golden vanilla ice with a layer of cake, sprinkle it well with $\frac{1}{4}$ cup of whiskey, and return to the freezer.

LANDSCAPE IN NORTHERN SPAIN *The greener areas of northern Spain are a source of the dairy products, particularly milk and cream, which figure in many desserts.*

For the white ice cream, beat the egg whites to soft peaks, then sprinkle with the sugar. Beat this 2–3 minutes, until the meringue has the gloss of high-quality satin. With the same beaters, whip the cream, adding the vanilla. Fold the meringue and cream together, cutting down with the edge of a big metal spoon 6–7 times. Remove the cake pan from the freezer and spoon the ice cream over the cake layer, smoothing the top. Slide the caramel disk on top, pressing it on very gently, and freeze overnight.

Carefully remove the sides of the cake pan and use a long narrow spatula to scoop up the coarsely chopped praline, pressing it onto the side of the cake. Slide it onto a serving plate. Whip the cream with 2 tablespoons of sugar and pipe rosettes on top around the edge, one on each portion. Dust each one with the last crumbs left from the praline. Return to the freezer until needed: a convenient party cake, it is soft enough to serve without any thawing. A sparkling Cava wine from Codorníu is just the thing to accompany it.

ROSCÓN DE REYES

TWELFTH NIGHT YEAST CAKE

Christmas presents come on Twelfth Night, January 6th, in Spain and it is not Father Christmas who brings them, but *Los Reyes Magos*, the three wise men, who arrived bearing gifts for Christ. This ornamental ring bread, eaten in the afternoon, has a little surprise hidden in it, formerly a single bean, similar to Provençal Twelfth Night cake.

Mesonero Romanos describes the scene as it used to be in *Un año en Madrid*, published in 1852. The cake is cut into equal slices and covered with a napkin "to avoid favoritism or cheats." Everyone is then given a slice, to the accompaniment of traditional songs. Whoever gets the *haba* or surprise is declared king of the festival and is in charge of entertainments during the evening. The king's last duty is to invite everyone to a feast on the following Sunday, at which time he relinquishes his kingship. The author laments that the custom has disappeared in Madrid (perhaps wives objected to this extra post-Christmas entertaining) and that the latter feast has become a breakfast or *merienda* – afternoon snack.

The festive bread in the picture was made with double the amount of dough. However, it was very difficult to handle and the recipe below, slightly adapted from Janet Mendel Searl's lovely book *Cooking in Spain*, is easier, though a food processor should not be used to knead the dough.

SERVES 10–12

2 packages active dry yeast
¼ cup sugar
6 tablespoons milk, warmed
2½ cups flour
½ teaspoon salt
1 teaspoon finely grated orange zest
1 teaspoon finely grated lemon zest
4 tablespoons butter, softened
2 large eggs
2 teaspoons dark rum
2 teaspoons orange-flower water
1 egg white, lightly beaten
¼ cup sliced almonds
candied fruit, including cherries, for decoration

Make a starter dough. Mix the yeast with 1 teaspoon sugar and the milk (at body temperature). Stir in 3 tablespoons of flour to make a wet paste. Let stand in a warm place – a gas oven with a pilot light, or the oven at its lowest setting (100° F) – for 20–30 minutes, until it is very frothy.

Meanwhile, sift the remaining flour with the salt into a large bowl and stir in the rest of the sugar and the orange and lemon zests. Cut in the butter until the mixture resembles fine bread crumbs.

Beat the eggs with the rum and orange-flower water. Make a well in the middle of the flour and add the eggs and the yeast starter. Use a wooden spoon to mix to a sticky dough. Then use one hand to slap the mixture backward and forward until it loses its stickiness. Be patient – even working vigorously the process will take at least 10 minutes, and is not successful in a food processor, where it becomes even stickier.

Transfer the dough to a lightly floured surface and continue slapping and kneading a further 5–10 minutes, until it is very smooth and elastic. Put the dough in a clean, oiled bowl, cover with a dish towel and leave in a warm place 1 hour until doubled in bulk.

Punch the dough down on a lightly floured surface to its original size. Slip in the *haba*, generally a little china rabbit or figure, or a coin, then shape the dough into a sausage that will fit snugly into a greased 9-inch springform tube pan. Cover again and let rise in a warm place 45 minutes.

Heat the oven to 350° F. Brush the top with lightly beaten egg white and sprinkle with almonds and candied fruit. Bake 30 minutes, until risen and golden brown. Let it stand 5 minutes, then push out of the pan and let cool on a wire rack.

ROSCÓN DE REYES

ENSAIMADA

MALLORCAN SWEET BREAD ROLLS

Halfway between a biscuit and pastry, these delicious sweet rolls are sent regularly from Mallorca to Barcelona, where they are a popular choice for breakfast. Their spiral shape is often compared to an Arab's turban, but I think it has a far older, and more feminine, origin in the *cabessal*. This is the spiral of twisted strips of cloth that is placed on a woman's head to enable her to balance a pitcher of water or basket. In Europe, it dates back at least to classical times, and only died out in nearby Languedoc in the 19th century. Larger *ensaimadas* are still made – the size of basket bottoms – and are sometimes decorated with a slice of the local *sobrasada* sausage.

Saim means "lard," which is traditional, but butter has replaced it, and it is used to separate the rings of bread as they expand. The recipe is a way of experiencing the old-fashioned pleasure that comes from handling bread dough.

MAKES 10 ROLLS

1 package active dry yeast
¼ cup sugar
½ cup milk, warmed
3 cups flour
½ teaspoon salt
1 extra-large egg
3 tablespoons sunflower oil, plus extra for greasing
2 tablespoons butter, melted
1 tablespoon honey
confectioners' sugar, for sifting

Make a starter dough with the yeast. Put it in a bowl with 1 tablespoon of sugar and the milk (at a temperature that feels neither hot nor cold to your finger). Stir in ½ cup of flour to make a smooth sticky cream. Put this in a warm place, such as in a gas oven with a pilot light, or the oven on the lowest setting (100° F), until it is very frothy and doubled in size, about 20 minutes.

Meanwhile, put the remaining flour, salt and sugar into a food processor. Or sift the flour with the salt into a large bowl and stir in the rest of the sugar. Beat the egg with the oil. Add the egg mixture and the frothy starter dough to the processor, or to a well in the middle of the dry ingredients. Process to a smooth elastic dough. Alternatively, use a wooden spoon to stir the two together, pulling the flour into the liquid. When a stiffish paste forms, switch to working with one hand. Knead the crumbs into the dough until it is a soft but not sticky ball. Flour a working surface lightly and knead the dough by pulling and stretching it, then slapping together again, until it is elastic and smooth.

Pull off egg-sized lumps of dough and roll each one out. With 8 fingers spread, roll it to and fro, moving the fingers outward until the roll is nearly as slim as a pencil, but twice the length. (The old way was to do this with hands coated in butter.) Pour the melted butter onto a plate and pass each roll through it, holding onto the ends. Tuck one end in and roll the sausage into a spiral, down onto a lightly greased baking sheet, then tuck the free end under so it can't come adrift. Leave plenty of room between the rolls. Cover the sheet with a dish towel and leave in a warm place about 1 hour, until the rolls have doubled in size.

Heat the oven to 375° F. Dissolve the honey with 1 tablespoon of hot water, then brush the rolls once. Bake 12 minutes, until pale golden brown. Remove them to a wire rack to cool, and brush them again with the honey mixture. Leave to cool 5 minutes, then dust with confectioners' sugar. Serve warm.

BRAZO GITANO

"GYPSY'S ARM" ROLLED SPONGE CAKE

The brown arms of the gypsy, perhaps raised with castanets in hand, provide the visual image behind the name of this long, thin sponge-cake roll, with its filling of chocolate custard, flavored with cinnamon and rum.

SERVES 6–8

SPONGE CAKE
butter for greasing
5 extra-large eggs
finely grated zest of 1 lemon
½ cup superfine sugar, plus extra for sprinkling
pinch of salt
⅓ cup flour

CREMA PASTELERA AL RON
4 oz semisweet chocolate, broken into small pieces
3 extra-large egg yolks
1 tablespoon flour
2 tablespoons cornstarch
¼ teaspoon ground cinnamon
1¼ cups milk, hot
½ cup sugar
½ teaspoon vanilla extract
¼ cup rum

Heat the oven to 350° F and line a jelly-roll pan with 15 × 10½ inches of parchment paper. Grease it well with butter. Separate the eggs, which should be at room temperature. Since most Spanish kitchens have temperatures in the 80s, I stand the bowl with the yolks inside a saucepan of hot tap water: this works very well if your kitchen is cool. Grate the lemon zest on your finest grater, using a little of the measured sugar to mop up the oil. Add the zest and about half the sugar to the yolks. Beat until they look like a thick pale custard, 2–3 minutes.

Beat the whites with the salt until soft peaks form. Gradually add the remaining sugar and beat to a glossy meringue. Fold the meringue into the egg yolks, cutting down with the side of a large metal spoon. Sift the flour over the top, a little at a time, and fold in.

Pour into the prepared pan and bake 12–15 minutes

BAKE SHOP *In addition to their delicious everyday fare, bake shops offer unique sweets for feast days, made only at that time of year.*

until pale brown and springy to the touch.

Have a sheet of parchment paper prepared and sprinkled with superfine sugar. Unmold the cake onto the sugared paper and remove the lining paper. Trim off the crisp edges and roll up from one of the long sides, with the sugared paper inside. Wrap it in a dampened dish towel and leave until cold.

Make the filling. Melt the chocolate in a bowl over simmering water, stirring occasionally. Stir the egg yolks, flour, cornstarch and cinnamon together to make a paste, adding a little milk if needed. Bring the milk and sugar to the boiling point, then pour onto the yolks, stirring. Return to the pan. Cook over low heat, stirring continuously, as the mixture is lumpy at first, until the custard is very thick and smooth. Off the heat, stir in the melted chocolate, vanilla and rum. Cover the surface of the custard with a piece of plastic wrap to prevent a skin forming and leave until cold.

Unwrap the sponge cake, spread with chocolate filling and re-roll. Wrap the paper around it until needed. Chill and serve the same day.

PASTEL VASCO

BASQUE CHERRY TART

This is the world's greatest picnic tart, for the heavy sweet pastry that the Spaniards love so well is perfect for eating outdoors. It has the texture and taste of sponge cake and is frequently cooked with a thick layer of custard in the middle. The earliest version of the tart was probably bread dough with a wild cherry jam inside, and cooked Morello cherries make the most delicious center. You can also use fresh black cherries, if these are available.

SERVES 6

2 cups flour, sifted, plus extra for rolling
1 teaspoon baking powder
pinch of salt
1 stick cold unsalted butter, diced
grated zest of ½ lemon
¾ cup granulated sugar, plus extra for sprinkling
2 medium eggs
1½ lb bottled or cooked Morello cherries in syrup, or 2 cans (16-oz) cherries, or 1 lb fresh black cherries

Put the flour, baking powder and salt into a food processor and work in the butter, or cut it in to make coarse crumbs. Add the lemon zest, using a little of the measured sugar to pick up the lemon oil from the grater. Work in all the sugar, 1 whole egg and the yolk of the second, to make a soft dough. Divide the dough into 2, one portion nearly twice the size of the other, and pat into 2 flat cakes. Put the dough cakes on plates and chill for at least 2 hours, preferably longer.

Heat the oven to 325° F with a baking sheet in it. Grease an 8-inch loose-bottomed tart pan. Leave the smaller piece of pastry in the refrigerator and roll out the larger portion on a floured work surface to 1 inch larger all around than the pan. Fold the pastry edges inward all around and slide the loose pan bottom under the pastry to pick it up. Put into position in the pan. This is a "press-in" pastry, so fit it evenly around the sides, without any trimming, so that it stands just clear of the top.

Remove the pits from the cherries, drain them and blot well on paper towels. Distribute the cherries in the pastry case, packing them in tightly. Roll out the pastry lid to fit inside the pan and position it on top. Fold the edge of the pastry case inward over the lid and press gently all around with a fork, just pulling the pastry away from the sides of the pan at the top.

Prick the lid in a few places, brush with the remaining egg white and sprinkle with a little sugar. Bake on the hot sheet 45–55 minutes until golden. Let the tart stand 5 minutes, then push upward out of the sides of the pan, and remove from the base. Let it cool on a wire rack.

MANTECADOS

CINNAMON SAND CAKES

Made all over Spain, these little dry cookies are closely related to *polvorones*, "crumble cakes." They combine flour, sugar and eggs, with an infinity of small local variations. In one town they might include a little ground almond, in another a glass of anise-flavored liqueur or the colorless *eau-de-vie, aguardiente*. *Mantecado* actually means "lardy cake," though they are more often made with butter. They are eaten for their texture, as a partner to dessert wine or ice cream, and almost never by themselves.

MAKES 12−15

1½ cups flour
⅔ cup blanched almonds
10 tablespoons unsalted butter, diced
¾ cup granulated sugar
½ teaspoon ground cinnamon

Heat the oven to 350° F. Spread out the flour on a baking sheet and toast until lightly colored − about 8−10 minutes. Toast the almonds in the oven for rather longer, until very lightly browned, then grind to a powder in a blender. Turn the oven down to 250° F.

Beat the butter with the sugar and cinnamon until creamy, then mix in the flour and almonds. Turn the dough onto a work surface − it is incredibly crumbly.

Pat into a mass about ½-inch thick, then cut out with an upturned sherry glass or a plain 2-inch cookie cutter. Move them carefully to a greased baking sheet and bake 30 minutes. Move carefully after baking, as they are very fragile. In Spain they are often wrapped.

Put a bowl of tangerines on the table and partner them with a glass of Scholtz Hermanos Solera 1885. A widely distributed Malaga dessert wine, this has a smell of walnuts about it, as well as the usual golden raisins. It is, nevertheless, not a wine to drink with desserts, because of its bittersweet edge.

ALMOND ORCHARD *Almonds were introduced by the Moors and remain an essential ingredient of many desserts.*

ALFAJORES

ARAB ALMOND SWEETMEATS

Medina Sidonia is a hill town with an astonishing view of Cadiz harbor in the distance, from which the commander of the Armada must once have watched Drake "singe the King of Spain's beard." Below the castle, in the town square, is a small shop selling an amazing assortment of traditional sweetmeats.

According to the Spanish epicure Luis Antonio de Vega, in *Viaje por La Cocina Española*, Medina Sidonia was "once the sweetmeat capital of the Muslim world. . . . In the 11th century the town exported cooks for the *seraglios* of the most opulent Muslim lords of Asia and Africa, some of whom, because they were women of great beauty, became the mothers of caliphs, kings and viziers – aided a little by the scents of their cooking pots." Naturally enough, the recipes are secret, but this is very close.

Honey and almonds are a favorite Arab combination and Spain specializes in single-flower honeys, like orange-flower. *Alfajores* make good Christmas candies rolled in colored papers, like *amaretti*.

MAKES 14–15

1 cup shelled almonds, including some unblanched ones
2 tablespoons dried currants
2⅓ cups fresh ground almonds
1 teaspoon ground cinnamon
½ teaspoon aniseed, roughly crushed
grated zest of ½ lemon
⅔ cup thick honey
confectioners' sugar for coating

Toast the whole almonds in a low oven (about 300° F), shaking the pan occasionally, until they are very lightly browned and give off a pleasant aroma (about 20 minutes), then chop coarsely. Snip the currants up in a cup with scissors, until very small.

Put the ground almonds, cinnamon, currants and aniseed into a bowl, adding the grated lemon zest, using a little of the ground almond to pick up the lemon oil off the grater. Warm the honey and stir into the mixture with a stout spoon. Add the chopped almonds and knead them in well with your hands. Before the mixture gets cold, pull off bits and roll them in a tray of confectioners' sugar to make small bullet shapes. Wrap each one in a square of colored tissue, twisting both ends. Black coffee and an orange liqueur like Triple Sec make a natural accompaniment.

MELOCOTÓN ASADO EN VINO TINTO

PEACHES BAKED IN RED WINE

Pears baked in red wine with cinnamon are well known; less well known is that they come from Galicia. Peaches in red wine are less familiar, and I first ate them in a monastery in Navarre, high in the foothills of the Pyrenees. Spanish table wines are cheap, fruity and uncomplicated – ideal for cooking. I look for Navarra wine, but it hardly matters.

Soft vanilla ice cream is the perfect partner. Try the white ice cream on page 128, which takes 2 minutes to make and needs no beating.

SERVES 6

6 large peaches
1 pint red wine, preferably Navarra
7 tablespoons granulated sugar

Heat the oven to 350° F. Choose a suitable container for baking the peaches, one in which they will fit tightly. Dip each peach in boiling water for 10 seconds, then skin them and arrange in the baking dish.

Heat half the wine with 4 tablespoons sugar, stirring to dissolve it. Add the remaining wine, bring to a simmer, then pour over the peaches. Bake, covered with foil, 30 minutes, basting once and spinning the peaches if they are not submerged. Sprinkle the tops with the remaining sugar and move to the top shelf, if your oven has the heating element at the top. Alternatively, slip under a hot broiler 2–3 minutes. Cool in the wine, then chill. Serve on glass dishes with a little pool of red wine on each one.

HORSE AND CART IN ARAGON *A traditional form of transport is used to carry the shopping home.*

FRESAS CON ANIS

STRAWBERRIES WITH ANISE

Strawberries are ripe just in time for Easter in Spain, and some of the most luscious berries are grown around Aranjuez, where the kings of Spain have the most beautiful summer palace. Chinchón, where one of the best brands of anise-flavored liqueur is made, is just a few kilometers away and this liqueur makes the ideal dressing for strawberries. In the south, a medium-sweet *oloroso* sherry is used for the same purpose; cream is much less common.

SERVES 4

1 lb (1½–2 pints) strawberries
¼ cup anise-flavored liqueur
2 tablespoons granulated sugar

Sprinkle the hulled berries with the liqueur and sugar and leave for "the time it takes to dance a *sardana*" – about 30 minutes. If the weather is very hot, serve on a glass plate, standing it in a shallow bowl of crushed ice.

EMPANADILLAS DE CIDRA

SWEET DEEP-FRIED PASTRIES

Skillet sweets, *dulces de sartén* are common in Andalusia, the best known being the *churro* rings that are made before your eyes in every market. The reason for frying them is simple. Houses traditionally have no ovens – it is simply too hot to use them so far south.

Empanadillas, which means "little pies," are the only sweet food sold in *tapas* bars. They usually have a shell marking on the outside, so may well be turned out by some sort of waffle iron. These homemade ones are smaller and are quite irresistible when newly made, so I have allowed 4 or 5 to a portion.

In the center of each one is Spain's favorite jam, called "angel's hair," *cabello de ángel*. It is made from *cidra*, an oval, melonlike squash, dark green but mottled yellow, which has very stringy flesh. Often the jam filling is omitted and sesame seeds are included in the dough instead. In this case they are called *borra-chuelos*, "drunken doughnuts," because they are then well dunked in the syrup.

SERVES 4

2 tablespoons sunflower oil
thinly pared zest of 1 lemon
2 tablespoons unsalted butter
½ cup white wine, not too dry
½ teaspoon aniseed (optional)
1¼ cups flour, plus extra for rolling
¼ teaspoon salt
⅓ cup "angel's hair," or another stiff jam
olive oil for deep frying
⅓ cup thick honey
2 tablespoons brandy
granulated sugar for coating

Heat the sunflower oil with lemon zest until it browns, then discard the zest. Add the butter, wine and aniseed, if using, and stir together. Remove from the heat and beat in the flour, with the salt, a little at a time until it forms a smooth dough. Remove from the pan and knead the dough briefly. Then let it rest in a plastic bag in the refrigerator for 2 hours.

Roll out the dough as thinly as you can on a floured surface. Traditionally it is then cut with a wineglass into 2½-inch circles. Spoon about ½ teaspoon of jam on one half; then with your finger dampen all around the edge with water and fold over in half. Seal the edges by pressing with a fork.

Heat fresh oil for deep frying. Make a syrup for dipping the doughnuts by melting the honey and brandy together. When a bread cube will crisp in the oil in about 40 seconds (top setting on an electric fryer), fry the pies, 4 or 5 at a time. They will usually bob to the surface when they start to expand. Spin them over with a slotted spoon and fry until golden. Drain on paper towels while you fry the next batch.

Dip the *empanadillas* into the syrup and place them on a wire rack. When they are all ready, transfer to a plate and sprinkle with sugar. Eat within half a day – if they last that long.

SANGRÍA

CHILLED WINE
AND CITRUS FRUIT PUNCH

At 4 o'clock on a hot summer afternoon, when the late lunch time customary in Spain is approaching, a pitcher of iced red wine and citrus fruit punch is the most welcome thing in the world.

SERVES 4

1 bottle red wine, chilled
6–8 ice cubes
juice of 2 lemons, plus 2 strips of zest
juice of 4 oranges
1½ pints soda water, chilled
2 tablespoons superfine sugar

Pour the wine over the ice cubes in a large bowl and add the strips of lemon zest. Squeeze the fruit juices, stir in the sugar and make up to 1½ quarts with soda water. Add this to the wine and serve in a large pitcher, glass or Spanish earthenware. Many Spanish shops sell one painted in blue with "*sangría*" on it.

EL CARAJILLO

BRANDIED COFFEE

The *guardia civil* no longer wear the shiny black patent leather hat, squashed at the back, that they did in Franco's time. But in country districts, they still patrol in pairs on motorcycles – chilly work in the mountains that make up so much of Spain. You can see them in bars, where so many people breakfast, having their morning drink of coffee and brandy before they set off.

SERVES 2

strong black coffee for 2
2 tablespoons Spanish brandy
sugar (for those who like it)

Make a good cup of coffee, *demi-tasse* size, and add a tablespoon of brandy, plus sugar if desired. Anis de Chinchón is also very good.

FARMHOUSE *A vine trained over the farmhouse wall provides fresh grapes for the inhabitants.*

INDEX

ACKNOWLEDGMENTS

The publisher would like to thank the following photographers and organizations for their kind permission to reproduce the photographs in this book:

3 Christian Sarramon; 6–7 Zefa Picture Library; 8 Guy Bouchet; 11–17 Retrograph Archive Collection; 22 Truchot/Explorer; 25 Truchot/Explorer; 29 Christian Sarramon; 30–31 Mike Busselle's Photo Library; 34 Pascal Hinous/Agence Top; 39 Carlos Navajas; 43 Anne Gael; 44 AGE Fotostock; 48–49 Mike Busselle's Photo Library; 50–51 Carlos Navajas; 52 Zefa Picture Library; 55 J N Reichel/Agence Top; 57 Zefa Picture Library; 64 J Ducange/Agence Top; 67 Anthony Blake Picture Library; 68–69 Mike Busselle's Photo Library; 74–75 Philippe Roy/Explorer; 79 Ted Funk/Agence Top; 86–87 Philippe Roy/Explorer; 89 Christain Sarramon; 91 Robert O'Dea; 96 John Downman/Hutchison Library; 97 Philippe Roy/Explorer; 101 Carlos Navajas; 105 Carlos Navajas; 110–111 Andrew Eames/Hutchison Library; 112–113 Mike Buselle's Photo Library; 116 Mike Busselle's Photo Library; 120–121 John Miller; 129 J Ducange/Agence Top; 133 The Anthony Blake Photo Library/Gerrit Buntrock; 135 Bernard Régent/Hutchison Library; 137 François Gohier/Explorer; 139 John Miller.

Special photography by Linda Burgess for Conran Octopus: 18–19, 33, 36–37, 40–41, 47, 60–61, 72–73, 76, 80–81, 84, 92–93, 98–99, 109, 114–115, 122–123, 126–127, 131.

Thanks to:
The Levant Trading Co., 10 Holland St., London W8 4LT
Gallery of Antique Costume and Textiles, 2 Church St., London NW8

The publishers would like to thank Cambridge University Press for permission to quote from *South from Granada* by Gerald Brenan.

BIBLIOGRAPHY

Colman Andrews, *Catalan Cuisine* (has Catalan bibliography, 1988) Marina Pereyra de Azar and Nina Froud, *The Home Book of Spanish Cookery* (1974) Luis Bettonica, *Cuisine of Spain* (En. ed. 1983) George Borrow, *The Bible in Spain* (1843) Gerald Brenan, *South from Granada* (1957) Elizabeth Carter, *Majorca Food and Cookery,* (1989) Penelope Casas, *The Foods and Wines of Spain* (1985), *Tapas* (1987) Elizabeth Cass, *Spanish Cooking* (1957) Alan Davidson, *Mediterranean Seafood* (1981), *North Atlantic Seafood* (1979) Hubert Duiker, *The Wines of Rioja* (1987) Richard Ford, *Handbook for Travellers in Spain* (1845), *Gatherings from Spain* (1846) Mary Hillgarth, *Spanish Cookery* (1970) Rudolf Grewe, *The Arrival of the Tomato in Spain and Italy: Early Recipes.* Journal of Gastronomy vol 3, no 2 summer 1987, Elisabeth Luard, *The La Iña Book of Tapas* (1989) Ana MacMiadhachäin, *Spanish Regional Cookery* (1981) Charles Metcalfe and Kathryn McWhirter, *The Wines of Spain and Portugal* (1988) Barbara Norman, *The Spanish Cookbook* (1971) Elisabeth Lambert Ortiz, *The Food of Spain and Portugal* (1989) Charles Perry, *Puff Pastry is Spanish*, Petits Propos Culinaires 17 (1984) Jan Read, *The Wines of Spain* (1982), *Mitchell Beazley Pocket Guide to Spanish Wines* (1988), *Sherry and the Sherry Bodegas* (1988) Jan Read and Maïte Manjón, *Flavours of Spain* (1978), *The Wine and Food of Spain* (1987) Alicia Rios, *The Cocido Madrileño: a Case of Culinary Adhocism*, Petits Propos Culinaires 18 (1984) Janet Mendel Searl, *Cooking in Spain* (1987) Victoria Serra, *Tiá Victoria's Spanish Kitchen* (1976) María José Sevilla, *Life and Food in the Basque Country* (1989) Marimar Torres, *The Spanish Table* (1986).

Francisco Abad y Maria Rosario Ruiz, *Cocinar en Navarra* (1986) La Condesa de Pardo Bazán, *La Cocina Española Antigua* (1912) Ana Maria Calera, *Cocina Castellana* (1980), *Cocina Balear* (1983), *Cocina Valenciana* (1983), *Cocina Vasca* (1987), *Cocina Catalana* (1988), *Cocina Andaluz* (1988) Jose Carlos Capel, *Manual del Pescado* (1982) E. Thibaut Comelade, *La Cuisine Catalane* (1981) Huguette Couffignal, *La Cuisine Rustique: Pays Basque* (1971) Alvaro Cunqueiro y Araceli Filquiera Iglesias, *Cocina Gallega* (has Galician bibliography, 1988) Maïté Escurignan. *Manuel de Cuisine Basque* (1982) Manuel Arroyo González y Carlos García del Cerro, *Quesos de España* (1988) *La Mejor Cocina Extremeña Escrita por las Dos Autoras Isabel y Carmen Garcia Hernandez* (1980) Josep Lladonosa Giró, *Cocina de Ayer, Delicias de Hoy* (1984) Gourmetour, *Guia Gastronomica y Turistica de Andalucía* (1988) Angela Landa, *El Libro de la Reposteria* (1988) Elviro Martinez Y Jose Fidalgo, *Cocina Asturiana* (has Asturian bibliography 1982) Manuel Martinez Llopis, *Historia de la gastronomia española* (has bibliography of historical cookbooks, 1989) Manuel Martinez Llopis y Simone Ortega, *La Cocina Tipica de Madrid* (1987) Lourdes March, *El Libro de la Paella y de los Arroces* (1985), Ines Ortega, *El Libro de los Huevos y de las Tortillas* (1986) Dionisio Pérez, *Guía de Buen Comer Español* (1929) Enrique Sordo, *Arte Español de la Comida* (1960) José Gutiérrez Tascon, *Cocina Leonesa* (1979) Luis San Valentin, *La Cocina de Monjas* (1989) Luis Antonio de la Vega, *Viaje por la Cocina Española* (1969).